# Just Take A Bite

## Easy, Effective Answers to Food Aversions and Eating Challenges

**Lori Ernsperger**

**Tania Stegen-Hanson**

**Just Take A Bite**

All marketing and publishing rights guaranteed to and reserved by

721 W. Abram Street

Arlington, TX 76013

800-489-0727

817-277-0727

817-277-2270 (fax)

E-mail: info@FHautism.com

www.FHautism.com



Printed in the United States of America



Cataloging in Publications Data is available from the Library of Congress.

ISBN #1-932565-12-4

# TABLE OF CONTENTS

# FOREWORD

## by Temple Grandin

Dr. Lori Ernsperger and pediatric occupational therapist, Tania Stegen-Hanson, take one of the most challenging problems in the family, that of a resistant eater and/or a child with food aversions, and offer a refreshing approach to expanding the child's repertoire of foods and create a balanced diet.

Their underlying theme is to understand the physiological, developmental, sensory and motor skills of the child and, most importantly, to respect the child's communication and response to eating. The authors attack many of the myths that surround eating, beginning with the idea that eating is a simple process. In fact, they contend and offer substantial proof that it's an incredibly complex process. They also dispel the "cultural myths" which surround food, one example being that parents are not doing their job well if their child doesn't eat "properly" or "clean his plate." Another is that problem eaters are "just being difficult," as if they're in a power struggle, when they often have underlying oral-motor delay or sensory integration dysfunction, allergies, or any number of other possible problems not yet identified. Some of the myths are actually life threatening, such as "If children are hungry enough, they will eat." Not so of some problem eaters, say the authors. The eating myths function as roadblocks to solving many problem eaters' selectivity and expanding their exposure to new foods.

The authors advocate a team approach to diagnosis, not only because of the technical components in problem eating, but also because if the child is in school or activities, it will take a team approach and time to expand the problem eater's diet. They enumerate a detailed list of various characteristics that act as indicators of the basic problems, to help the reader in making careful observations and assessment. They also provide exercises for the parents and professionals to examine their beliefs and eating experiences so the child may begin a healing process.

Once the problem that is often the bane of many families' existence is identified, the authors explain how to design and implement a comprehensive treatment plan. The treatment plan offers refreshing relief from past behaviors because the authors address specific recommendations, and their approach is " to focus on the child" and "to have fun with food and not just focus on eating or putting food in the mouth." They advocate introducing one new food item to the problem eater with each meal while always having at least one of the preferred food items present. The authors discuss setting up the correct environment, providing support for physical and oral-motor needs, and creating a myriad of games for playing, touching, smelling and even painting with food, among other activities, to encourage enjoyment of the physical components of eating (the mouth) and eating itself.

This talented team has a blockbuster book, literally and figuratively, as they offer a positive program to help those who are struggling at least three times a day with the serious problem of food aversion and food selectivity.

# ACKNOWLEDGEMENT

## by Lori Ernsperger

I must first acknowledge all of the children and parents who have shared their eating experiences with me. I hope this book can assist you in your journey of learning and loving new foods.

This book was improved immeasurably by the thorough editing and skill of Kirsten McBride. Kirsten was able to take the ramblings of two authors and create an outstanding manuscript with a singular voice and purpose. I also appreciate the many hours of hard work put forth by Victoria Ulmer and Wayne Gilpin at Future Horizons. The entire staff at Future Horizons have encouraged and supported this project in various ways. I would also like to thank Dr. Kay Toomey who first taught me about the eating challenges faced by children with developmental disabilities.

Finally, I would like to thank my husband, Tom Ernsperger, for his endless support and love of eating. This book is dedicated to our children, Ben and Jessica, who provide the basis for my wonderful and challenging experiences in parenting. My husband and children endured many meals which included experimenting with new and exotic foods.

I thank you all.

# ACKNOWLEDGEMENT

## by Tania Stegen-Hanson

God has blessed me with the following very important people who have enriched my life and made my contribution to this book possible:

Dave, my husband. I thank him for his support and understanding when a lot of time was spent in front of the computer or meeting with Lori. I am grateful that he is my partner and my friend, and words cannot begin to express how much he means to me.

My wise, wonderful parents, Emil and Sonja. Even though so many miles separate us, their love and support is always felt. Their encouragement never wavered.

My colleague and friend, Susan Holden, who had to keep the practice going when I traveled for further training or when I had to work at home to meet a deadline. The dictionary defines the word friend, but Susan demonstrates it.

Lori, without her vision, passion, dedication and unstoppable determination, I would have never had this opportunity to co-author this book. As a first-time author, I could not have asked for a better experience—she encouraged me, tried at all times to relieve my workload, taught me so much, and along the way became my friend.

Suzanne Evans Morris, my mentor, with whom I had the privilege of spending a week of training in Virginia. I am so grateful for her insight and wisdom and the countless hours spent reading my emails, replying to them and for reading the book and providing valuable suggestions and comments.

Last but not least, I thank the children and parents with whom I've had the privilege of working. Thank you for allowing me into your lives and around your dinner table.

# INTRODUCTION

Sharing a meal with family and friends can be a most rewarding and life-affirming activity. There is nothing more satisfying than a lazy morning brunch, a picnic in the park, going to a new ethnic restaurant, or lunch with friends in the school cafeteria. In most cultures, sharing a meal with family and friends is the cornerstone of celebrations and holidays.

Eating and sharing a meal is a wonderful experience unless you are a resistant eater or you have a resistant eater in your family. Then eating and mealtimes are often stressful, chaotic, and involve constant negotiation. Mealtimes and celebrations can soon turn disappointing over unfulfilled expectations and dashed hopes when a resistant eater refuses to share a meal with family and friends.

Eating is often perceived as a simple process. Just put the food in your mouth, chew, and swallow. But that is a myth. Eating is an incredibly complex process that can be challenging for many individuals. It requires the cooperation and coordination of all the bodily systems. A number of things can interfere with a child's oral-motor development and feeding patterns. Whether you are the parent of a resistant eater or a professional working with a resistant eater, it is extremely important to seek appropriate treatment for eating challenges.

Providing support and assistance for resistant eaters is important for a variety of reasons. First, resistant eaters can permanently impair their long-term growth. Children identified as resistant eaters often have a low percentile for weight and height. Second, a lack of an adequate, balanced diet can interfere with a child's ability to learn properly and, therefore, progress academically. Thus, without sound nutrition and adequate vitamin intake, resistant eaters are limiting their potential in the classroom. Third, for some resistant eaters starvation and hospitalization can occur. Although most people believe children will "eat when they are hungry," a small percentage of them will not eat, which eventually may lead to hospitalization for malnutrition and starvation. Lastly, problems with eating can impact a child's socialization and self-esteem. Eating and socialization are closely connected. Eating is an important socialization skill and builds a sense of belonging. Many cultures, including the United States, include eating as part of their holidays and celebrations with family and peers. Resistant eaters are often isolated from their families during mealtimes and may not fit into their mealtime environments. Considering the risks involved, parents and professionals cannot overlook this issue or rely on outdated treatment methods. Problems with eating is a serious issue that requires a comprehensive multisensory treatment approach.

The number of food items selected for eating and the amount of foods consumed by an individual can be viewed on a continuum. Resistant eaters are on the extreme far end of the eating continuum. We all have food preferences, and some of us may be considered picky eaters. But resistant eaters go far beyond the typical "picky eater" on the food eating continuum. Some of these children and adults eat fewer than five different foods, and some refuse entire food groups.

Resistant eaters are a mixed group, who exhibit a myriad of characteristics. Some resistant eaters have medical issues or physical impairments. Others have a sensory integration dysfunction that makes them overly sensitive to smells and textures, or poor oral-motor skills and may not have developed appropriate tongue control, chewing, and swallowing skills. Resistant eaters may also include individuals who have been diagnosed with autism or other developmental disorders. There is not one single characteristic to identify resistant eaters. In

Chapter One we will review the specific characteristics for resistant eaters to assist parents and professionals in determining the extent of a child's problem.

It is difficult to estimate the number of children who experience food aversions and eating challenges. So far no thorough study within the medical, educational, or nutritional fields has determined the exact prevalence rates of this population. However, studies have focused on specific groups of children. For example, several studies have shown that nearly 80% of children with severe mental retardation have feeding difficulties and inadequate diets (e.g. William, Coe, & Snyder, 1998). According to Mayes and Calhoun (1999), 75% of children diagnosed with autism spectrum disorders experience atypical feeding patterns and have limited food preferences. Approximately half of the autism population studied were hypersensitive to textures and lumps in the food. Further research on problem eating was conducted by Lorna Wing (2001), who reported that nearly two-thirds of the 230 children with autism spectrum disorders in her clinic experienced problems with food, which included limited food diets and severe food fads. Finally, it has been estimated that nearly 45% of typically developing children experience some level of eating problems during childhood (Bentovim, 1970). Without a well-funded research study to address the prevalence rates, we may never know the exact number of children and families who suffer with pediatric eating problems and often do not receive the necessary help.

Although we do not know the exact prevalence rates of the various kinds of resistant eaters, the treatment techniques presented in this book target the full continuum of resistant eaters and picky eaters. That is, children along the eating continuum from far less severe eating challenges to serious food aversions, can benefit from these effective and common sense strategies with great success.

Before we proceed, we want to caution parents and professionals who are working with children with severe medical and physical needs. This book is not intended to address some of the severe feeding issues and physical difficulties associated with tube feeding. Some children with severe physical and medical limitations require significantly more than the treatment plan suggested here and are clearly beyond the scope of this book. For further information on this topic, refer to Suzanne Evans Morris and Marsha Dunn Klein, *Pre-Feeding Skills: A Comprehensive Resource for Mealtime Development, 2nd ed.* (2000).

Addressing the needs of resistant eaters is a collaborative effort between parents and professionals working with the child. Although parents are the primary caretakers, classroom teachers and other professionals can play an important role in the treatment plan. Much of the information presented here is directed towards parents, but this book is also designed for school professionals and clinicians. Addressing the behavioral, physical, and sensory needs of a child who is a resistant eater requires a multidisciplinary team, including the parents, for a successful treatment plan. A collaborative team approach will ensure the plan is implemented across settings and throughout the child's day. This book outlines specific goals and objectives that can be achieved across settings including the home, classroom, or a therapy setting. Because of the often negative experiences the child has experienced at the dinner table, the classroom or therapy room is often a neutral environment conducive for exploring new foods.

*Just Take A Bite* was written to provide parents and professionals with a comprehensive treatment plan for addressing food aversions and problems experienced with eating. It is our hope that the practical strategies and suggestions in this book will enable you to create a friendly family and school environment for exploring new foods. In order to accomplish this, this book will:

- Define the characteristics and criteria of a resistant eater
- Review typical oral-motor development and the stages of eating
- Describe how sensory integration dysfunction can compromise the child's performance at mealtimes
- Identify the factors contributing to resistant eaters
- Present specific oral-motor activities
- Develop a comprehensive treatment plan
- Review the fundamentals of how to create positive mealtime environments
- Provide sensory lesson plans for exploring new foods

In order to assist the reader in internalizing the strategies suggested in this book and therefore use them more effectively, we have created a series of activities called "An Exercise in Eating" that are interspersed throughout the chapters. Take some time to complete these exercises. Each activity is designed to allow you to reflect on your beliefs about eating and to experience mealtimes from the perspective of a resistant eater.

Solving the mealtime dilemma is not a quick fix. A comprehensive plan requires both families and professionals to make a commitment to the child. It is our hope that after reading and implementing the strategies in this book, you will feel empowered with appropriate treatment strategies for supporting the needs of resistant eaters. For most parents, the goal of any eating program is to "get the child to eat more food." Although increasing the child's number of foods is an important secondary goal, the main focus of this book is to provide children and families with a positive mealtime environment and support them as they explore new foods. In addition to increasing children's food selections, the broader target for this program is to change mealtimes from stressful to relaxing and fun. Our goal is to support family connectedness by respecting and nurturing the child beyond diet and food choices.

Although this book is filled with many common sense tips, practical strategies, and lesson plans, the best approach is to follow your heart. Ask yourself at meals and when eating: Does this feel right? Is this meal enjoyable for everyone? Sometimes we have to step back and allow the child to lead us into learning about new foods. Adults working with a resistant eater must facilitate, guide, and be partners with children at mealtimes.

# CHAPTER ONE

## Who Are Resistant Eaters?

*It's a typical night in the Jenson family. Mom has just gotten off work and collected her two children, Logan and Daniel, from day care. Logan is eight and Daniel is four years old. As Mrs. Jenson walks in the front door, she is already feeling stressed about tonight's dinner. Mr. Jenson will be home for dinner tonight and Mrs. Jenson wants the family to sit down at the dinner table for a meal. When dad is working late, usually mom is a short-order-cook making the boys whatever foods they prefer. Although Logan is considered a good eater and will eat a variety of foods, Daniel is a resistant eater.*

*Tonight's menu will include pork chops, mashed potatoes, and carrots. These are not items Daniel will typically eat. Daniel has a long history of not eating and is small for his age. Prior to the meal ever starting, Daniel begins to complain about the awful smells coming from the kitchen and starts his ritual of pacing around the family room, complaining very loudly about the upcoming meal.*

*As the family sits down to dinner, both Daniel and his parents feel stressful and anxious. Daniel's dad believes strongly that Daniel is just being difficult and should be forced to eat his meal. Mrs. Jenson would like to see Daniel just try the pork chops, but she knows he will gag and scream if they force him to eat. The tug-of-war at the dinner table has been going on for years. On this night like many others, Daniel is sent away from the table as a punishment and mom will end up making him a special snack later in the evening before he goes to bed.*

This evening meal at the Jenson home is typical of families with children who have been identified as resistant eaters. The term "resistant eater" will be used throughout this book to describe children similar to Daniel. Resistant eaters such as Daniel are not "just being difficult" or noncompliant, they often have an underlying oral-motor delay or sensory integration dysfunction that causes them to limit their food selections. For example, Daniel is a perfect example of a child who is experiencing an increased gag reflex, which contributes to his inability to eat new foods. Over sensitivity to strong smells may also be inhibiting his willingness to eat. Mr. and Mrs. Jenson are caring parents who are using the parenting skills passed down to them from prior generations and readily supported in western culture. While they are very loving and want what is best for their son, they simply do not have the necessary skills or training to address food aversions and food selectivity in a proactive manner. This type of problem eating can be pervasive and emotionally challenging to families and professionals, however, with a thorough assessment and a written comprehensive treatment plan stressful mealtimes such as these can change for both Daniel and his parents.

**Identifying a Resistant Eater**

Resistant eaters like Daniel are a heterogeneous group not defined by a single test or diagnosis. Due to the variety of defining characteristics of resistant eaters, a multidisciplinary team, including the parents, should utilize a variety of methods for determining the extent of eating difficulties. There is not one defining assessment tool or a single diagnostic criteria for identifying resistant eaters. Typically developing eating patterns and resistant eaters can be viewed on an eating continuum:

| **Normal Eaters** | **Picky Eaters** | **Resistant Eaters** |
|---|---|---|

Children develop eating skills and food preferences at varying rates and to varying degrees throughout childhood. That is, eating is a developmental process which changes over time as the child becomes more confident with his or her eating skills. Many children between the ages of two and three years old are picky eaters because they are going through a stage of development where they fear new foods. In children with developmental delays this stage may occur at a later age. This fear of new foods improves during childhood. As children enter adolescence they may again begin to select a more restricted diet and their eating schedule will change.

These changes in childhood are normal and most children balance their food selections and eat a nutritional diet over a period of time. Children with normal eating patterns are often judged as "good eaters." Ellen Satter (1999), describes a good eater as someone who, "likes eating, is interested in food, feels good about eating, and likes a lot of different foods" (p. 179). Not all children are good eaters and some children are described as "picky eaters." Although picky eaters have certain limitations and aversions to foods, they eventually eat enough of a variety of foods to maintain a balanced and healthy diet. Resistant eaters, however, are on the extreme end of the eating continuum and have serious food aversions and or medical impairments that prevent them from eating a balanced diet.

### Common Characteristics of a Resistant Eater

Although resistant eaters are a mixed group with a variety of characteristics, for the purpose of this book, the term "resistant eater" applies to any individual who meets the following characteristics:

| **Table 1.1** *Characteristics of a Resistant Eater* |
| --- |
| **Resistant eaters often exhibit one or more of the following:** |
| 1 Limited food selection. Total of 10-15 foods or less. |
| 2. Limited food groups. Refuses one or more food groups. |
| 3. Anxiety and/or tantrums when presented with new foods. Gag or become ill when presented with new foods. |
| 4. Experiencing food jags. Require one or more foods be present at every meal prepared in the same manner. |
| 5. Diagnosed with a developmental delay such as Autism, Asperger's Syndrome or Pervasive Developmental Disorders-Not Otherwise Specified. May also have a diagnosis of mental retardation. |

### 1. Limited Food Selection

One of the most distinguishing characteristics of resistant eaters is their overall limited food selection. For some resistant eaters, this number may be 20 different foods; for others, it may be as few as 3 foods. Examples of limited foods often include chicken nuggets, pizza, yogurt, or macaroni and cheese. It is not uncommon for most of the selected foods to have similar traits, such as being white, having similar textures, or being easy to chew. Other resistant eaters may be limited to foods that are pureed or they demand a bottle or baby food passed the recommended age.

***Kelly***

Kelly is a typical four-year-old in every way except that she is a resistant eater. As reported by her mother, Kelly only eats about seven different foods. Kelly's mom remembers she had difficulty transitioning Kelly from baby foods to finger foods. Although her parents attempted a variety of tactics to get her to eat, Kelly refuses to eat any new foods. Kelly will eat bananas, chicken nuggets, bread, cheese crackers, and scrambled eggs. Her parents have tried everything to get her to eat new foods, but have been unsuccessful.

Kelly is like most resistant eaters, who select a limited food diet. She also selects foods that have similar traits. Most of the foods Kelly selects lacks color and are extremely bland in taste. Limited food selections are the trademark of a resistant eater.

**2. Limited Food Groups**

In addition to a limited number of foods, resistant eaters also limit the food groups they will eat. Some resistant eaters only eat from one food group, such as breads and cereals. Most resistant eaters love carbohydrates, such as French fries and macaroni, often omitting foods from the fruit and vegetable group and/or meat group.

***Ben***

Ben is a six-year-old male who is a resistant eater. He was diagnosed with autism when he was three years old. Ben has made excellent progress in his educational program and is entering a full-day general education first-grade class with educational supports. But although he is doing well in many areas, he is limited in his diet. Ben refuses all vegetables and will only eat an occasional hot dog or chicken nugget from the meat group. He eats mostly dairy products and carbohydrates. Ben's mom is concerned about his eating because next year he will be in school all day and will be required to eat in the cafeteria. Although she will be sending his lunch, she is concerned about his ability to focus and learn throughout the day due to his limited diet and his refusal to eat from a variety of food groups.

Ben's selection of foods is typical for a resistant eater. Resistant eaters often refuse foods from certain food groups. Although Ben will occasionally eat a hot dog or chicken nugget, these foods do not provide a balanced diet. Limiting intake from food groups such as fruits and vegetables can have a significant impact on the child's overall health and cognitive growth and learning.

### 3. Averse Reaction to New Foods, Which May Include Tantrums and/or Gagging

Anxiety, tantrums, and stress-related symptoms are typical behaviors exhibited by children who are resistant eaters. As we will explain in Chapter Three, food neophobia refers to a fear of new foods. Neophobia is a developmental stage for typically developing two- and three-year-olds. Although most of us experience some levels of food neophobia, resistant eaters typically have an extreme reaction when presented with new or novel foods that continues even as they grow older. Resistant eaters may exhibit their fears through anxiety, tantrums and/or gagging when presented with a new food.

***Juan***

Juan is a seven-year-old male with severe food aversions. Juan has mild cerebral palsy. He is in a regular second-grade classroom. He receives physical and occupational therapy in school. Juan has had difficulty with new foods since he was an infant. His parents report that he had food allergies and was not willing to accept new foods. Juan's teacher notes that Juan is a good student but exhibits anxiety and stress when there are new foods in the classroom. He also has trouble with some of the smells in the cafeteria and goes to the nurse's office during lunch to avoid eating food from the cafeteria. His parents report that they cannot go to different restaurants because Juan becomes ill and cries when surrounded with new smells.

Juan's reaction to new foods is often experienced by resistant eaters. Some resistant eaters have highly sensitive olfactory systems that can impair their willingness to tolerate new foods. The olfactory system assists us when smelling foods and is an important part of normal eating. Crying, gagging, and even vomiting are often reported by parents and professionals when a resistant eater is forced to eat a new food, due in part to a hypersensitive olfactory system.

## 4. Food Jags

A food jag is defined as the insistence on eating the same foods in the same manner over long periods of time. Food jags limit opportunities for the resistant eater to experience new foods and eat a balanced diet. Food jags are common in young children and usually change over time. For example, a typical three-year-old may request peanut butter and jelly every day for weeks but will eventually switch to macaroni and cheese and then back to peanut butter and jelly. Resistant eaters, on the other hand, will food jag and eventually satiate on a particular food and refuse that food item in the future.

***Mackenzie***

Mackenzie is a four-year-old with a limited diet. She currently eats only 10 different foods and has had several food jags over the years. Mackenzie insists on the same yogurt and peanut butter sandwich every day for lunch. Not only does she request the same items, she also insists that they be the same brand name of yogurt and peanut butter. Mackenzie's parents report that she had a similar food jag with chicken nuggets and bananas and now refuses to eat either food. They are concerned that if in the future she refuses to eat the peanut butter and yogurt, she will only be eating eight foods.

Although food jags can be part of normal eating development, parents and professionals should be cautious if the food jag continues for more than a few days. The longer the child is allowed to eat the same foods each day, the less likely she is to increase to a variety of foods in the future. Parents and professionals should encourage learning about new foods on a daily basis as recommended in Chapter Nine.

## 5. Developmental Delays and Other Medical Diagnosis

Countless neuromuscular disorders, developmental delays, and medical diseases can interfere with chewing, swallowing, and digestion. A large percentage of resistant eaters experience health-related disorders that may permanently impair their eating development. Cerebral palsy, mental retardation, and muscular dystrophy are just a few of the disorders that can contribute to problems with eating. If a child has been diagnosed with a medical disorder, doctors and other professionals often address the main issues related to the primary diagnosis, frequently leaving parents with little support or knowledge to address the secondary issues of problems with eating.

***Quince***

Quince is a three-year-old male who was born six weeks premature. He was on a feeding tube for several months as an infant and was not transitioned to a bottle until nine months of age. After several more months, Quince was diagnosed with failure to thrive. His parents have visited a variety of pediatricians and gastroenterologists looking for answers to their questions about Quince's inability to eat. At the age of three, Quince has been also diagnosed with a developmental delay. He appears unable to eat any solid foods and his parents are still feeding him junior-level baby foods.

Quince and his family have experienced a great deal of stress and anxiety due to his medical problems and developmental delays. Although his parents have attempted to find the answers to his eating difficulties, they have been unable to locate a professional with adequate knowledge about addressing the needs of resistant eaters. Developmental delays and other medical diagnosis can significantly impair a child's ability to eat properly.

Each of the characteristics listed in table 1.1 are common to resistant eaters. The list is not exhaustive and not every resistant eater will exhibit each characteristic. A feeding team, including the parents, should review each item and identify the nature and extent of the problem for the individual child.

**Food Neophobia Scale**

The characteristics for determining a resistant eater presented in table 1.1 is a simple tool that can be used by both parents and professionals. If further assessment is needed to determine if the child is a resistant eater, The Food Neophobia Scale (FNS), developed by Pliner and Hobden (1992), may be used. Food Neophobia is the fear of new foods. The FNS is a simple 10-item questionnaire that parents or a professional can administer or complete themselves. The FNS was designed to predict a person's willingness to try new foods and his or her level of food neophobia. Typically developing two- to four-year-olds experience food neophobia for short periods of time. But by the age of five most children have decreased their fear of new foods and are willing to try new and novel foods.

According to Pliner and Hobden (1992), a score greater than 35 is considered high. Such a score is one indicator that a child is a resistant eater and may benefit from a comprehensive treatment program. The Food Neophobia Scale is a helpful tool in assessing resistant eaters as resistant eaters often share traits similar to those of individuals who experience food neophobia.

**Table 1.2** ***Food Neophobia Scale***

*Mark the following when answering items 2, 3, 5, 7, & 8

1=disagree extremely
2=disagree moderately
3=disagree slightly
4=neither agree nor disagree
5=agree slightly
6=agree moderately
7=agree extremely

****Mark the following when answering items: 1, 4, 6, 9, & 10 (bold and italics)***

1=agree extremely
2=agree moderately
3=agree slightly
4=neither agree nor disagree
5=disagree slightly
6=disagree moderately
7=disagree extremely

____ **1.** ***I am constantly sampling new and different foods.***
____ 2. I don't trust new foods.
____ 3. If I don't know what is in a food, I won't try it.
____ **4.** ***I like foods from different countries.***
____ 5. Ethnic food looks too weird to eat.
____ **6.** ***At dinner parties, I will try a new food.***
____ 7. I am afraid to eat things I have never had before.
____ 8. I am very particular about the foods I will eat.
____ **9.** ***I will eat almost anything.***
____ **10.** ***I like to try new ethnic restaurants.***

* If parents are rating their child, change each item to include "my child"

The FNS is not recommended as a single assessment tool to determine problem eating but should be used in conjunction with the previous listed characteristics and other assessment tools.

**Other Assessment Tools**

It is important for the multidisciplinary team of professionals, including the parents, to review all pertinent information and assessment data with regard to the individual child who is experiencing problems with eating. As with all assessment procedures, it is recommended that a team complete a thorough medical history before determining the need for a feeding program. The team may also want to complete further assessment if a child is exhibiting oral-motor delays. Parents of school-aged children may access school professionals for further assessment. Speech and language pathologists and occupational therapists are highly trained in the area of oral-motor delays and assessment. A multidisciplinary team should examine the individual child's eating patterns across environments and investigate inconsistencies in the child's diet.

| **Table 1.3** *Considerations for Assessment Outcomes* |
|---|
| 1. Extent of problem eating |
| 2. Environmental factors |
| 3. Physical impairments |
| 4. Oral-motor delays |
| 5. Sensory impairments |
| 6. Medical history |

It is important for a multidisciplinary team to have a complete understanding of the child's medical history and any other contributing factors for problem eating in order to create an individualized comprehensive treatment plan.

## Conclusion

A multidisciplinary team can utilize a variety of approaches to identify a resistant eater. Reviewing common characteristics and completing the Food Neophobia Scale and other oral-motor assessment tools are just a few measures available to parents and professionals. Parents of resistant eaters often note that "they know a resistant eater when they see one." Resistant eaters are usually significantly different than their typical peers due to the amount of stress and anxiety they experience around new foods. However, although the problem may be readily apparent, it is still important to complete a thorough assessment in order to ensure the team is aware of the child's strengths, weaknesses, and medical history. Individualized assessment allows parents and professionals to identify the exact nature of the problem and determine if there is a significant physiological delay. A thorough review of the child's history and assessment of oral-motor delays will assist the team in writing a comprehensive treatment plan.

# CHAPTER TWO

## Oral-Motor Development

The term oral-motor skills refers to the movements of the muscles in the mouth, lips, tongue, cheeks, and jaw. Oral-motor skills include the functions of sucking, biting, crunching, chewing, and licking. To perform effective eating, it is necessary that the child has adequate oral-motor skills. Oral-motor skills are not only dependent on the muscles of the mouth for effective functioning. A child with poor oral-motor skills often demonstrates:

- Delays in development of motor skills
  - Low muscle tone
  - Poor postural control
  - Poor balance and coordination (difficulty running, jumping, catching and throwing a ball)
  - Difficulty crossing the midline of the body—we cross the midline when we read from left to right or rub an elbow (i.e. unable to use one side or part of the body—such as a hand, foot, or eye—in the space of the other side or part)
  - Difficulty using both sides of the body simultaneously (i.e. difficulty carrying a tray or a plate of food, tying shoes and opening a lunch container)

- Difficulty with eye-hand coordination (i.e. bringing spoon to the mouth, coloring, drawing, cutting and writing)
- Decreased awareness of where the body is in space (i.e. bumps into furniture, people and obstacles in the environment)

■ Problems with speech and language development

- Using facial expressions (this is hard for children with poor oral-motor skills because the muscles in their face and mouth do not work well.
- Inappropriate use of inflection when speaking
- Inadequate breath control when speaking
- Speaking either too loud or too soft

■ Difficulties paying attention and organizing behavior

- Unable to calm him/herself
- Struggling to transition from one activity to another in a calm manner
- Inflexible attitude toward daily routines

Oral-motor skills have a very important influence on the child's overall development. For example, poor oral-motor skills may lead to the following feeding and eating problems:

■ Gagging or frequent choking

■ Drooling

■ Difficulty keeping food down and digesting food

■ Difficulty transitioning to different textured foods

■ Difficulty sucking, chewing and swallowing

- Picky eating habits, strongly preferring certain food textures, temperatures and tastes while avoiding others

This chapter provides an overview of how oral-motor and feeding skills develop from birth through the first three years. Our intent is to highlight important stages in the child's oral-motor and feeding development, so the reader can identify at which stage of development the resistant eater's skills are. Knowledge of feeding and oral-motor developmental sequences provides the parent, teacher and therapist with the building blocks for creating treatment programs.

***Sarina***

Sarina's mother reports: "Sarina didn't start on solid foods at the same stage that her peers did. She didn't seem to know how to chew the food; she didn't even seem to know that the food was in her mouth. We were afraid that she might choke, so we continued giving her pureed foods for a long time. By the time she started eating solids, she did not want to eat any foods that required a lot of chewing—sticking to the soft, mushy foods. Sarina is now six years old and she has a very limited diet and refuses to eat protein-rich foods such as chicken or meats or any foods that require a lot of chewing."

A child's developmental readiness determines when to introduce solids, when to introduce different textures and how the feeding is done. It is important to be aware of a child's developing mouth patterns (oral-motor skills) as well as hand and body control, so you know what intervention is appropriate with regard to food texture and feeding techniques.

When assessing Sarina, her developmental history revealed important factors that her mother had not even thought of as a new parent. For example, Sarina did not explore toys using her mouth, she drooled excessively as a baby and because she preferred soft, mushy textures, her mother fed her until the age of three when Sarina learned how to feed herself with a spoon. She only touched biscuits and crackers, which would dissolve in her mouth. Sarina's occupational therapy assessment findings revealed low muscle tone and poor postural control; hypersensitivity to touch, especially around her face and inside her mouth; poor eye-hand coordination; poor handwriting skills and poor eating skills, which were further compromising her organization of behavior. She hated changes in routine, especially at mealtimes, and tried to avoid all challenging activities such as playground games or handwriting assignments. Sarina's mother reports that being a first-time mother, she was not aware of the red flags during her daughter's development. "If I had known what I know now, I would probably have sought an assessment and intervention for Sarina earlier in her life."

The following overview contains general information to guide the reader. It does not include all the intricacies of oral-motor and feeding development. For more involved analysis of oral-motor and feeding development, the reader is referred to Chapters Four and Five in Suzanne Evans Morris and Marsha Dunn Klein's book, *Pre-Feeding Skills: A Comprehensive Resource for Mealtime Development, 2nd ed.* (2000). Keep in mind, all children develop at their own rate. In addition, these skills may develop more slowly in a child with a disability.

## In Utero

By the third month of gestation, the baby can be viewed on ultrasound images as sucking the thumb and swallowing amniotic fluid. The baby is starting early in life to learn how to use the muscles and movements she will need for eating and for calming herself.

## Newborns: 0-3 Months

***Adam***

Adam and his mother were exhausted. Adam, two months old, would take an hour to drink 1-2 ounces. Adam's mother was not getting rest because she had to feed Adam every hour in order for him to get enough food. He was not gaining weight. His mother had tried to breastfeed but had been unsuccessful. When Adam drank from the bottle, he demonstrated a noisy, inefficient suck and erratic breathing, and a lot of the milk would end up on his chin and clothes. He appeared to work hard at feeding, but after a few minutes he would look exhausted and his mom had a hard time preventing him from falling asleep. She knew that he would wake up after a 5 to10 minute nap screaming because he was hungry again. An oral-motor assessment revealed that due to Adam's weak lips and cheeks and a weak tongue, he was working harder than necessary to form a lip and tongue seal around the nipple of the bottle. Furthermore, he was struggling to coordinate his breathing and swallowing. Inefficient suck-swallow-breath pattern caused Adam to fatigue easily.

A newborn is dependent on his caregiver for positioning during feeding. Initially babies are inclined and on their side during breastfeeding. There are multiple benefits to positioning a newborn in an inclined position for feeding. First, this position allows the head and body to be in better alignment; second, if there is too much breast milk in the baby's mouth, the fluid automatically drains out from the lower cheek; and third, the jaw and tongue can move without having to work as much against the pull of gravity.

A newborn baby usually drinks 2-4 ounces of liquid every three to four hours (the amount is determined by the child's weight). The lips, tongue, and jaw work together to form a seal around the nipple during drinking. The newborn is able to coordinate his sucking with his breathing into what is known as the suck-swallow-breath rhythm.

*ORAL-MOTOR SKILL ACQUISITION AT THIS AGE:*

- Oral reflexes are present for protection and survival.
- The tongue appears flat and cupped.
- The jaw, tongue, and lips move as one unit. They do not move independently from each other.

Babies put their hands in their mouth, suck or mouth their parents' fingers, the edge of a blanket, their clothes or pacifier, and other objects that come into contact with their mouth. This is known as *generalized mouthing*. Through this type of mouthing, babies familiarize themselves with general sensations of softness, firmness and hardness. Exploring these sensations creates important learning opportunities to prepare the child to transition to the sensations of a nipple to a cup and a spoon.

**4-6 Months**

At this age, the child is able to sit with support, has good head control, and uses her whole hand to grasp objects (called the *palmer grasp*). The infant frequently puts her fingers, clothing and anything else in her hand, to her mouth, for sucking and mouthing.

Greater control of the head allows the four to six-month-old to feed in a more upright position (45° to 90°). A child at this age requires four to six feedings (7 or 8 ounces of liquid per feeding) daily.

*ORAL-MOTOR SKILL ACQUISITION AT THIS AGE:*

- Up-and-down munching movement of the jaw develops. Munching is the earliest form of chewing. The tongue flattens and spreads as the jaw moves up and down.
- The baby is able to transfer food from front to back of tongue to swallow.
- Easy tongue protrusion occurs when swallowing.
- Gag reflex diminishes.
- Soft, smooth solids are introduced by spoon between four and six months. The baby recognizes the feel and look of the spoon.
- Swallowing is accomplished by a suckle-swallow movement, or by a simple protrusion of the tongue at the point of swallow.
- Between six and seven months, the infant is able to open her mouth and hold it stable as

the spoon approaches. The lower lip pulls in to remove food. This allows for the upper lip to be able to develop more precise movements for clearing food off the spoon.

The mouth continues to play the primary role in sensory discovery. That is, the world is discovered through the mouth as the child begins to explore an object by taking it to the mouth.

**7-9 Months**

During feedings, the child is typically sitting in a high chair. To sit securely, he may need some external support such as rolled towels, pillows or a lap tray. He is able to follow the food with his eyes. He begins to use his thumb and index finger to pick up objects (this is called the pincer grasp), and thus begins to feed himself with his hands.

*ORAL-MOTOR SKILL ACQUISITION AT THIS AGE:*

- The infant's lips show lateral closure, which means that they can close tightly at the corners.
- Jaw movements are separate from tongue and lip activity. The early suckle pattern still predominates, but is mixed with more frequent up-and-down tongue movements that eventually emerge into the more mature suck pattern.
- The sides, center, and tip of the tongue begin to differentiate in the process of collecting and swallowing pieces of lumpy foods.
- The child is able to transfer a piece of food from the side to the center of the tongue and conversely, from the center to the side of the tongue.

- The child begins to eat ground or finely chopped food and small pieces of soft food. She begins to experiment with a spoon but still prefers to feed herself with her hands.

By exploring toys with their tongue, lips and jaw, children find out about size, shape, surface texture, taste and weight. This stage, called *discriminative mouthing*, is important as it familiarizes the child with the sensory features necessary when encountering solid foods. In this way, the child expands his/her sensory awareness and discrimination, learns to move smaller pieces of food around, and swallow safely. During teething, sensations from the gums draw children's awareness to their mouth, and the desire to place things in the mouth becomes greater. In this way, the child learns about sensations that increase comfort, and increase biting and chewing skills.

**10-12 Month-Old**

At this age, the child starts to develop good eye-hand-mouth coordination as demonstrated in his ability to hold a cup up to his mouth and to put a spoon in his mouth independently.

*ORAL-MOTOR SKILL ACQUISITION AT THIS AGE:*

- The child may continue with the bottle or breast at bedtime, but takes liquid primarily from the cup.
- Upper incisors are used to clean food from the lower lip when it is drawn inward.
- Lip closure while swallowing liquids and solids is common.
- The child uses a well-controlled and graded bite. By 12 months, the child has no

difficulty eating foods with lumps, and he/she can separate the lumps that are ready to be swallowed from those that require more chewing.

- A controlled bite is used through a soft cookie. Success of biting through hard cookies will depend upon the presence of teeth and the ability to control the force of the bite.
- The one-year-old is able to learn to suck through a straw.
- The child starts to eat coarsely chopped food and small pieces of soft, cooked table food or easily chewed meats.

At age one, children are very active, enthusiastic participants during mealtimes. Due to their growing desire for independence, they try to feed themselves by drawing any cup, spoon, or food to their mouth, often spilling as much on the floor or on themselves as they get into their mouths.

**13-15 Month-Old**

The toddler is able to sit in a high chair or stool so that she is at the right height at the table. A high chair with foot rests, can also help her stay confined, so she can keep her attention on the eating experience and have her feet supported at the same time.

*ORAL-MOTOR SKILL ACQUISITION AT THIS AGE:*

- Drinking skills are now more refined. Less spilling occurs during drinking and when the cup is removed.
- Children are able to use smooth, well-coordinated diagonal movements of the jaw

during chewing. (This chewing pattern gives the impression that the jaw is moving diagonally.)

- The cheeks help the tongue keep the food over the grinding surfaces of the teeth with greater skill.
- The corners of the lips and the cheeks draw inward to assist in controlling the placement and movement of food in the mouth.
- The tip of the tongue is able to lift up independently to explore the roof of the mouth and front palate. This pattern may not develop while the child is on a spouted cup because the spout lies on top of the tongue, preventing the tip of the tongue opportunity to lift up.
- Choking and coughing rarely occur as long sucking sequences are used to drink an ounce or more of liquid.

By 15 months of age, the child is able to control his/her drooling when attempting newly acquired gross-motor skills such as walking and running. Some drooling may occur if the child is cutting teeth, however.

**16-18 Month-Old**

The 18-month-old is able to sit unsupported at the family table or at a small chair and table. The highchair is no longer needed for safety and security. Children can feed themselves using their fingers or a spoon and can drink from a cup independently.

*ORAL-MOTOR SKILL ACQUISITION AT THIS AGE:*

- There is minimal loss of food during chewing.
- When drinking liquids from a cup, the child uses external jaw stabilization by biting the rim of the cup.
- The upper lip moves downward, contacting the edge of the cup for improved skill in drinking.
- Swallowing occurs with easy lip closure and with an elevated tongue-tip position.

There is better overall control of food and liquid with minimal spillage or loss of food during eating.

**19-24 Month-Old**

By two years of age, the child has acquired the foundation for skilled eating patterns. Two-year-olds eat independently and engage in advanced fine-motor tasks such as manipulating small objects and two-word speech combinations without drooling.

*ORAL-MOTOR SKILL ACQUISITION AT THIS AGE:*

- The tongue cleans the lips.
- Child can transfer the food across the midline of his tongue.
- The child can drink from a straw.
- Loss of liquid when drinking from a cup is rare.

By 24 months of age, the types of food eaten vary because of personal tastes and preferences—not usually because of a lack of coordination and skill.

### 25-36 Month-Old

The refinement of oral-motor control during feeding continues as the child's mouth continues to change in shape and size and as the child loses and then gains new teeth.

*ORAL-MOTOR SKILL ACQUISITION AT THIS AGE:*

- The child uses tongue to clean the area between gums and cheeks.
- The child grades jaw opening for different thicknesses of food.
- The child is able to chew her food using three chewing patterns:
  a. Her jaw moves directly up-and-down in a vertical pattern.
  b. Her jaw moves up-and-down in a diagonal pattern.
  c. Her jaw swings from the center to the side of the mouth where the food is located, and without a pause, the jaw swings smoothly towards the other side of the face, helping the tongue carry the food to the opposite side. Because of the circular swing that the jaw makes, this chewing pattern is called a "circular rotary" movement.

Children need to be provided with many opportunities to explore and to practice their newly acquired skills. In addition, they must be developmentally ready to move to more complex levels of eating and drinking. It is important for parents and professionals to recognize the stages of oral-motor development and know at what age the child should start acquiring each oral-motor skill.

It is important to wait to start solids until the child is ready. The child has to learn so much at once. She has to learn to eat from a hard, cold spoon instead of the usual soft nipple, she has to figure out how to get what is on the spoon into the mouth, and then she has to figure out how to move this food around inside her mouth and make it go down the throat, swallowing it, without gagging on it. For this reason, a child is started on a pureed diet. As the child acquires more complex oral-motor skills, she is able to manage a greater variety of textured food.

**Food Texture and Eating Skills**

"Texture" refers to how smooth, lumpy, thick, or thin the food is. The following table describes different textures, examples of food, and what oral-motor skills are necessary for the child to be able to handle a given texture. They are listed in order of increasing difficulty level.

| **Table 2.1** | ***Food Texture*** | | |
|---|---|---|---|
| **Texture** | **Description** | **Example** | **Child can** |
| **Thin puree** | Food forms a thin paste or thin liquid; use strainer or blender and blend to a paste, add liquid for thinner consistency | Cream of wheat, pudding, applesauce; blended meats, vegetables and fruits; commercial baby food | Suck and swallow; take food from spoon with lips |
| **Thick puree or blended** | The transition into thicker smooth foods seems to be an important step for many infants and children with feeding issues. Food forms a thicker consistency or heavy "mash" that doesn't have lumps. | Blended meats, vegetables and fruits. (Gerber will be bringing out the beginnings of their revised 3rd food line.) | Suck and swallow; take food from spoon with lips; swallow thickened puree and not gag |
| **Mashed lumpy** | Foods form a heavy bolus (a soft mass of chewed food); food is blended or mashed with a fork; food retains some texture and consistency | Mashed potatoes; mashed bananas and other soft fruits; mashed hard cooked eggs; mashed carrots or squash | Swallow without gagging; close lips while swallowing food; remove food from spoon with lips; up-and-down munching movement |
| **Ground** | Food ground in food chopper, not blended; food retains some lumps for chewing foods; should be easy to chew 1/8 to 1/4 inch in size | Crumbled/ground meat; scrambled eggs; cottage cheese; small pieces of toasted bread crusts; crackers broken into small pieces | Begin to chew in rotary pattern |
| **Chopped** | 1/4 to 1/2 inch in size | Fruit cocktail | The above, plus side-to-side tongue movement and vertical and diagonal jaw movement, with enough strength to break up the pieces |
| **Regular** | Cut up food or leave it whole | All foods | Close lips and keep food in mouth; bite through food; enough jaw strength to grind |

Once children have developed a new oral-motor skill, they learn to select which eating movement to use based on the sensory feedback they receive from the food, the environment and the utensils used.

***Nicole***

At the age of 15 months, Nicole was still eating only pureed baby foods. At twelve months of age, her mother tried to offer her finely mashed table food. She gagged and refused to open her mouth for more. Based on this initial response, her mother went back to giving her only smooth, soft foods. During an evaluation of Nicole's feeding skills, the therapist placed a small piece of graham cracker in the center of Nicole's tongue. Nicole's tongue did not move the food to between the teeth for chewing. Instead, Nicole held her mouth closed and waited for the graham cracker to dissolve, and then she sucked on it. Based on normal oral-motor development, a child develops the skills to chew a soft cookie between 6 and 9 months. Since Nicole does not demonstrate other developmental problems, it may be assumed that she had no experience with anything that would stimulate her latent chewing abilities. When given the sensory stimulus of a more solid piece of food, she uses the sucking strategy that she is familiar with. When the therapist placed the graham cracker on the side of the mouth, Nicole began to mash it between her gums. After a bit of practice, her tongue started to move the food to the side and she began to chew the cracker.

## Conclusion

A review of the child's oral-motor development and eating history is crucial to gaining a better understanding of the child's experiences and reactions to eating and drinking. A child is only able to eat food when she is developmentally ready. Forcing and coercing children to try new foods when they do not know how to manage it in their mouths, will lead to the child refusing to eat and attempting everything in her power to avoid the eating experience. Therefore, building on the child's oral-motor strengths and introducing foods when the child is developmentally ready, will lead to more positive mealtime experiences. Chapter Three will discuss how environmental stressors, cultural beliefs and behavioral factors can contribute to a child's aversion to eat.

# CHAPTER THREE

## Environmental and Behavioral Factors Contributing to Problems with Eating

As mentioned earlier, the simple and relaxing activity of eating a good meal is often taken for granted. As a nation who enjoys eating, we assume all children will automatically learn to eat and enjoy all foods. If eating issues arise, it is most likely that the family's pediatrician will advise a wait and see attitude. As a result, the seriousness and frequency of problem eating often go undetected and untreated for years. Thus it is usually not until the child grows out of the toddler stage and problem eating persists that parents and professionals begin to question the child's food aversions. In general, the medical, educational and nutritional fields lack a thorough understanding of the causes of resistant eaters and effective intervention strategies.

Many factors may contribute to problems with eating and food aversions. For some children physical, neurological, and sensory impairments inhibit the willingness and ability to try new foods. Other children may experience neophobia, or fear of new foods. Stressful mealtime environments and cultural beliefs about eating can also significantly affect a child's eating patterns and food selections. A few of the most common factors contributing to food aversions and food selectivity discussed in this chapter are:

- Food neophobia
- Environmental factors
- Cultural roadblocks
- Developmental disabilities and mental retardation

Often a combination of factors is contributing to the food aversions and food refusal experienced by a resistant eater. In the following, we will examine the major contributing factors listed above.

**Food Neophobia**

As mentioned in Chapter One, food neophobia, a fear of new and novel foods, has long been recognized as a developmental stage for children between two and three years of age. A young toddler who is transitioning to adult foods will be offered a variety of new foods. During this period, children often reject a new food at first glance. The reaction of the child experiencing food neophobia however will be more severe including signs of distress and anxiety towards a new food. Unfortunately, the novel food is often removed by the parent, who perceives the child as rejecting the new food. Most parents are unaware of this developmental stage and may limit the variety of foods offered to the child based on apparent fears and rejection.

***Samantha***

Samantha is a typical two-year-old who is learning to eat new foods. Samantha's parents have been providing a variety of new foods at dinner. Unfortunately, Samantha screams and cries when a new vegetable is placed on her plate. Her parents quickly remove the cause of her frustration replacing it with green beans, a vegetable she has grown accustomed to. Over time, Samantha has come to eat only one vegetable: green beans. Her parents do not want to cause her or themselves any further stress and anxiety, so they limit her exposure to new vegetables.

Neophobia should diminish as the child approaches five years of age. As with any developmental stage, some children become extremely rigid and do not outgrow this fear of new foods. For some children, this fear of new foods may last through adulthood. Children who have not been given adequate exposure to new foods may eventually become adults who reject new foods.

***Sequoias***

Sequoias is a 29-year-old woman with a full-time career in banking. She has had a lifetime of eating problems. Although Sequoias is considered to be of average height and weight, she eats an extremely limited diet of carbohydrates and a few proteins. She recalls many family dinners during childhood when she was the last person at the table, staring at a plate of vegetables and mashed potatoes. Sequoias, who comes from a traditional family, was forced to "clean her plate." Unfortunately, she never received

*Sequoias cont.*

any treatment to address her eating problems. As a result, she is now an adult with poor eating habits. Although Sequoias understands the nature of her problem, she continues to be reluctant to eat new foods even at parties or restaurants.

Many children and adults, like Sequoias, do not develop past this neophobic stage. Some resistant eaters remain in this stage due to cognitive or developmental delays. They may also experience difficulties with other developmental milestones such as speech and oral-motor activities. If left untreated, this group of children with developmental delays may experience food neophobia throughout their lives.

*An Exercise in Eating*

Try something new! Go to the grocery store and purchase one item you have never eaten before. Maybe it's a new and exotic fruit or vegetable. Or try eating a new kind of seafood. Bring home your new item and start exploring it. How does it smell, feel, and taste? Be present with the new food item. How do you feel? Are you eager or anxious to try this new food? Consider your reactions to the new foods as they may be similar or different than what is experienced by a resistant eater.

Although food neophobia is a typical developmental stage for two- and three-year-olds, it should not be left untreated if it persists. The child will end up with a limited diet if parents continuously remove the foods that are causing fear and anxiety. As will be discussed in Chapter Nine, continuous exposure to a variety of new foods helps the neophobic child overcome fear and broadens food selections.

## Environmental Factors and Eating

Environmental factors play a key role in developing and maintaining food aversions and problem eating. It is not unusual for our daily lives and family mealtime environments to be chaotic and stressful. Environmental stressors can develop from a variety of sources, including chaotic work schedules, cultural beliefs around eating, and the diagnosis of a developmental disability. Family schedules and mealtimes have become increasingly chaotic as children have become involved with more extracurricular activities and parental work schedules are more varied than in the past. Unpredictable mealtime schedules contribute to problems with eating. Thus, problems with eating are exasperated when children do not have a consistent schedule for meals or if they are allowed to graze on unhealthy foods throughout the day. Hunger and appetite are prerequisites to healthy eating and a balanced diet. If the child is unsure of the schedule for snacks and dinner, it is difficult for him to regulate hunger and satiation.

Not only is the mealtime schedule important, the setting of the meal can also affect healthy eating habits. Families "on the go" often supplement meals with snacks in the car or stop by a local fast-food restaurant for a quick meal. More and more children are eating their meals in front of the television or roaming around the house eating snacks. Recently a parent from a food clinic explained, "Jeremy was more compliant when eating dinner while watching his favorite video. So, I set up a picnic table in front of the television."

These choices of mealtime settings limit the child's exposure to a balanced diet and opportunities to improve his or her socialization skills. As will be discussed in Chapter Seven, one of the first steps to treatment for resistant eaters consists of designing and implementing a mealtime schedule and providing a consistent and supportive setting.

***Jonathan***

Jonathan's family is a typical family of the 21st century. They have baseball practice three times per week after school and swimming classes on Fridays. Both parents work fulltime and Dad puts in a lot of overtime. This kind of schedule may not be problematic for most families, except nine-year-old Jonathan is a resistant eater. He does not eat any meats except for chicken nuggets, and the only vegetable he will eat is raw carrots. He rejects most fruits but will occasionally eat a banana, if there are no brown spots. As Jonathan and his family go through their week, they usually sit down for dinner as a family on Sundays. During the rest of the week, mom is a "short-order-cook" offering individual frozen meals selected by Jonathan and his brothers. Jonathan's mom is stressed and too tired to battle food fights every evening.

This scenario is familiar to families across the country. Nevertheless, most parents and children will receive a balanced meal throughout the week—except for resistant eaters. Unfortunately, these environmental factors will continue to support a resistant eater's food aversions and limit overall food intake.

**Cultural Roadblocks**

One of the most challenging factors contributing to a resistant eater is cultural beliefs regarding food and mealtimes. We all have a personal belief system about foods and how to eat properly, that has been passed down from generation to generation. Most parents typically do not receive training when it comes to resistant eaters, so they often fall back on the rules and beliefs their parents instilled in them when they were growing up. Unfortunately for resistant eaters, these rules and beliefs often interfere with their ability to experience new foods and broaden their diets. The following is a list of the common, yet damaging rules and beliefs for eating:

1. **Good parents are responsible for getting their child to eat.**

   From birth through the first six to eight months, parents appear to have complete control over what their child eats and how much. As the child becomes more independent, the responsibility for eating rests squarely with the child. Ellyn Satter, in her book, *How to Get Your Kids to Eat...But Not Too Much (1987)*, provides parents and professionals with an important message called the "Division of Responsibility":

   *"Parents and professionals working with children are responsible for preparing and providing a balanced meal at an appropriate schedule and setting. The child is solely responsible for whether they eat and how much they eat."*

   Parents from traditional households often believe they are responsible for making sure their child eats adequately. Thus, many parents resort to coercing or forcing their children to eat. "You cannot leave this table until you finish your spinach!" Or, "No TV tonight if you don't finish your chicken." While such threats appear to work for children who do not have eating challenges, coercion and punishment do not work for resistant eaters. Force feeding generates negative emotions, which are then associated with mealtimes. Force feeding also causes a physiological response called "fight or flight." Each of us has a fight-or-flight response when we are being coerced or bullied. When this occurs, our appetite is naturally suppressed in order to allow our bodies to escape the environment or fight back. Thus, contrary to their intentions, parents who use coercion and feel responsible for making sure their child eats are actually suppressing the appetite of their child.

***Amanda***

Amanda is a charming six-year-old with an extremely limited diet. According to her mother, Amanda eats fewer than 10 foods and demands pizza at every meal. Amanda can be extremely noncompliant at the dinner table, by screaming when presented with new foods. Her parents have tried a number of strategies to "get her to eat," including forcing her to eat and putting the food in her mouth against her will. Not surprisingly, the dinner time environment in the family has become very stressful. Her parents are beginning to argue about the best methods to make Amanda eat her dinner. Mom is tired of fighting every night at dinner, but Dad is not willing to give up that easy. As a father, he feels responsible for getting Amanda to eat. The family is clearly struggling with the best approach.

Amanda's parents are very typical of many cultural beliefs. Parents are the dominant force when it comes to creating mealtime environments, and therefore they often assume the responsibility for getting their children to eat. This belief is a cultural roadblock for children who experience problems with eating.

Not only do resistant eaters have a fight-or-flight response, they also become distrustful of their parents which limits their capacity to have a positive experience when learning to eat new foods. Mr. Garcia, a father of a resistant eater, recently reported that his son refused to come to the dinner table. After further investigation, Mr. Garcia admitted that once the child got to the table, the meal was often fraught with stress and coercion. Most meals were spent talking about what the child was eating and whether the child had eaten enough. Every meal in the Garcia household was focused on the resistant eater. Naturally, the child began to refuse to come to the table.

As with the Garcia family, many parents become more concerned with getting food into the child's mouth than with the child himself. In order to create a positive mealtime environment, parents and professionals must focus less on the food and more on the child's experiences at the table and learning about new foods.

2. **Don't play with your food!**

We have all heard our parents tell us not to "play with our food." Most cultures have strict rules about using the proper utensils and many do not tolerate eating with one's fingers.

Not only are we to use specific utensils for certain foods, we are to sit properly and chew with our mouths closed. Many families still believe eating is a solemn occasion and that it should not include playing with food. One mother reported seeing her son Jeff, a resistant eater, playing with grapes on the table. She quickly reminded him, "If you are not going to eat them, don't touch them."

Although implementing good manners at the table is an appropriate skill to teach most children, these same restrictions can create a roadblock for resistant eaters. Playing with foods and eating with one's fingers is the first step to learning about new foods. As will be discussed in Chapter Nine, many resistant eaters require tactile or touching opportunities to experience new foods prior to putting them into their mouths. If parents and professionals are uncomfortable with playing with food during mealtimes, they can provide opportunities for playing with food during other times of the day and away from the dinner table.

3. **If children are hungry enough, they will eat. Children will not starve themselves.**

A popular daytime talk show host recently presented his views on "picky eaters" stating that "children will eat when they are hungry." He went on to say that "children will not starve themselves." Finally, he suggested that "picky eaters" are in a power struggle with their parents and that parents need to "win the battle over food."

Although this type of mentality is common, it is a roadblock for resistant eaters. Most typically developing children eventually eat when they are hungry. But due to the nature of resistant eaters, if parents continue to force them to eat new foods before they are ready, they will continue to reject those foods. Indeed, some resistant eaters will starve themselves and jeopardize their health and weight. Thus, approximately 4-6% of resistant eaters will starve themselves and require medical intervention (Toomey, 2002). Also, some resistant eaters have other developmental delays or sensory integration dysfunction and do not understand the signals for hunger. These children can go several days without eating. Although this talk show host was providing adequate strategies for the majority of picky eaters, it is unreasonable to expect resistant eaters to follow these guidelines.

4. **Don't talk with your mouth full.**

Another tried-and-true rule for eating dictates not talking with one's mouth full. Again, this may be an important rule for Miss Manners, but it ultimately hinders the eating ability of some resistant eaters especially those with delays in oral-motor development. In fact, parents of resistant eaters are encouraged to talk with their mouths full in order to be role models for their children. Resistant eaters often have oral-motor delays and therefore, do not have adequate skills to manage the process of chewing and swallowing. Parents and professionals who are eating with children who are resistant eaters should take the time to describe how they chew and where the food goes in the mouth. They can also teach the purpose of the teeth in chewing and how the tongue is utilized to move the food around in the mouth.

All of these important skills can be modeled and cognitively explained to the child who may be struggling with eating. Our first goal is to focus on improving the overall diet and food selections of resistant eaters. After meeting that goal, parents and professionals can begin to work on table manners.

5. **Sweets and desserts are rewards for eating your meal: "You can't have dessert, if you don't eat your meal."**

At a recent luncheon during a training session with a group of adults, dessert was placed on the table prior to the start of the meal. All of the adults in attendance followed an unspoken rule and politely ate their sandwiches before starting on the tempting cake. Although no one spoke this rule aloud, not one person touched the cake until they finished eating.

Our culture perceives sweets and desserts as a reward for eating one's meal. You rarely find a family that starts the meal with a piece of chocolate cake, nor do you hear parents saying, "If you don't eat your ice cream, you can't have any salad." Instead we are much more likely to hear parents tell their children, "If you don't finish your carrots, you can't have any cake." This type of emphasis on desserts puts an inordinate amount of attention to sweets. A resistant eater will interpret this as, "I have to eat the bad food in order to get the good food." For parents of resistant eaters, it is better to incorporate a small amount of dessert into the meal and not set any stipulations for the child to receive dessert. All foods should be considered on the same priority level with the same amount of importance.

6. **Certain foods are for breakfast while other foods are for lunch and dinner.**

   Another roadblock within our culture is the belief that certain foods are for certain meals. When was the last time you had green beans with your breakfast or had cereal for dinner? Most of us have categorized certain foods for each meal of the day. Although adhering to these categories is not damaging to most people, for resistant eaters these rules limit their exposure to new foods.

   As will be discussed in Chapter Nine, repeated exposure to new foods is a critical step in treatment for resistant eaters. If parents and professionals continue to limit the variety of foods at each meal, the number of exposures will also be limited. Also, resistant eaters usually follow very rigid rules when they eat. Categorizing foods to certain meals provides resistant eaters with more rules to follow. "I can't eat cucumber slices with breakfast!" Such personal beliefs can be challenging to change.

7. **Leaving food is wasteful; clean your plate. "Do you know how many children are starving in Africa?"**

   The tradition of the "clean plate club" began as a World War I campaign to conserve food due to a limited supply. Clearly outdated, this message perseveres. Being part of the "clean plate club" is still encouraged in many families. Parents believe they have fulfilled their responsibilities when the child has eaten the last bite of food on the plate. Indeed, family members will comment on "what good eaters" children are when they have finished off the last morsel of food.

Unfortunately, this standard of eating is harmful to children who are resistant eaters. First, portions provided to children are often grossly oversized. Even the size of the plate used for young children is too large. Parents often scoop adult-size portions of food on a large dinner plate and place it in front of the child with the expectation they will clean their plates. Second, not only does the child have too much food on his plate, he is encouraged to eat quickly. The pace of the meal can be overwhelming to a child who has oral-motor delays and struggles with chewing and swallowing. And finally, forcing children to eat beyond when they are satiated distorts their ability to naturally control their diet. A child might ask the parent, "Can I be done?" and the parent usually responds, "Just take one more bite." Children are born with an innate ability to control their food intake and balance their diet. Unfortunately, our culture encourages overeating, "biggie sizes" and cleaning your plate. As parents and professionals, we must start small and encourage children to stop when they are full.

Our personal and cultural beliefs are ingrained into our daily lives through our family relationships and the media. Letting go of our personal and cultural beliefs is extremely challenging. The message often given to parents and children is that eating is easy and that bigger is better. Due to societal standards, parents of resistant eaters are often embarrassed or ashamed that they cannot get their child to eat.

***Stephen***

It was the first parent meeting for a summer food clinic addressing food aversion and food selectivity. Stephen's parents sat in the back, quietly taking notes, as the program was reviewed. Stephen's mother shared that he was eating fewer than 10 items and regularly refused to eat with the family. The guiding philosophy of the food clinic is that eating is the responsibility of the child and we have to address our personal beliefs about foods and eating before we can help others who have problems with foods. Stephen's father quickly replied that he was able to "get" Stephen to eat by threatening to take away his Nintendo or revoking his privileges to swim. Therefore, he was not willing to sign up for an eight-week intensive food program to address his son's food aversion. In short, Stephen's father was not ready to let go of his perceived parent responsibility of making his child eat.

Stephen's father is a good example of the difficulties we experience in overcoming our personal beliefs and cultural roadblocks. This parent was caring and well intentioned but continued to be guided by the premise that eating can be coerced and parents are responsible for making their child eat. For many families of resistant eaters, it requires hard work and dedication to address these cultural roadblocks that must be removed in order to move forward on the road to recovering from problem eating.

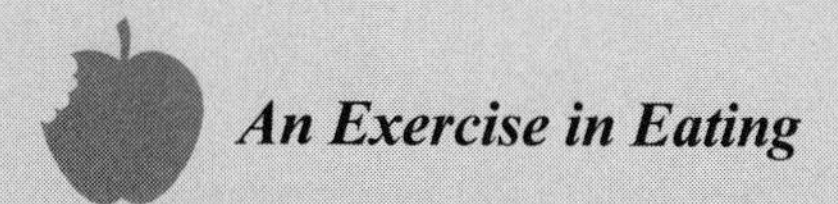

*An Exercise in Eating*

Depending on your own culture or geographical area, you may know of other roadblocks.

Write down a list of your beliefs. Include in your list any beliefs not listed above.

**Resistant Eaters and Developmental Disabilities**

Many childhood disabilities and disorders contribute to problem eating and hinder the eating process. Mental retardation, cerebral palsy, autism, and Asperger's Syndrome are just a few disabilities which may interfere with the normal development of eating a balanced diet. As mentioned in the introduction, there is a high correlation between problem eating and children with disabilities. The specific characteristics surrounding these disabilities contribute to problems with eating. For example, sensory integration dysfunction, immature respiration, and delayed oral-motor development cause difficulty with normal eating. Limited communication skills, rigid behaviors, and routines may also be factors.

The characteristics and symptoms associated with pervasive developmental disorders (PDD) and mental retardation (MR) can hinder normal eating development. Characteristics such as limited communication skills, restricted and rigid behaviors, and cognitive delays are factors that may interfere with the child's acquisition of new foods.

1. **Limited communication skills are closely linked with food aversions and food selectivity.** Although there is much debate about the interconnectedness between eating and speech, many clinicians believe there is a causal relationship. Thus, children who experience speech delays, due to immature oral-motor development, also experience difficulty with oral-motor control necessary for eating new foods. There appears to be a strong correlation between early sound production and the necessary muscular control required to develop appropriate eating skills. Children diagnosed with PDD and/or MR also have delayed speech and, subsequently, are more likely to become resistant eaters.

   As reported in Chapter One, nearly 75% of the autism population has severe food aversions. Although we do not have any scientific data to support or deny this causal relationship between resistant eaters and impaired communication skills, it requires a closer review. When creating a treatment plan, parents and professionals are instructed to include oral-motor activities for any child experiencing food selectivity or speech delays.

2. **Restricted patterns of behavior and repetitive routines are often associated with PDD and can also be found in other disabilities**. The child may become obsessed with the packaging of a food or with a particular plate and spoon.

*Carlos*

Carlos was diagnosed with autism when he was 30-months-old by a neurologist. He displayed many of the typical autism characteristics such as delayed speech, impaired socialization, and stereotypical patterns of behaviors. Carlos also exhibited severe food aversion. He would only eat with his dinosaur plate and spoon. He screamed and cried if mom changed to a different package of his favorite juice box or cooked the "wrong" kind of macaroni and cheese. Carlos was also rigid about standing up when he ate his meals. Any attempts at getting him to sit down at the table with the family created a tantrum. Carlos' parents were frustrated with his rigid eating demands.

The type of rigidity displayed by Carlos is common in children with PDD. The nature of the disability creates inflexible routines and rigid food patterns. Children with mental retardation and other disabilities may share these traits. A comprehensive treatment plan should apply the necessary steps in addressing these problems.

3. **Cognitive delays and mental retardation can interfere with the development of appropriate eating skills.** One problem may be the child's inability to associate hunger with eating. Some children with disabilities experience hunger but are unable to associate that feeling with food.

Parents of children with a disability may experience a variety of emotions and grief over their child's diagnosis. When a child with a disability is diagnosed at a young age, the family is often stressed and confused. The emotional turmoil of having a child with a disability may limit a parent's ability to cope with the initial eating problems and food aversions. When parents are feeling stressed and anxious, they are less likely to provide a mealtime environment that is supportive and structured. Some parents of children with disabilities become overprotective and limit any demands on their child for eating a balanced diet. Due to stress and anxiety, these well-intended parents provide a special diet to appease the child and limit further health problems.

***Dillon***

Dillon was born premature and had several surgeries before he turned two years of age. He is now three-years old and in the 20th percentile for height and weight. Dillon's parents have spent the last three years struggling to keep him healthy and out of the hospital. Because of his medical problems, Dillon has been given food supplements and maintains a diet of mostly pureed foods. Although his physician is confident Dillon can transition to a more typical and varied diet, his parents are cautious. They have attempted to provide him with meats and vegetables but Dillon cries and refuses to take a bite. Dillon's parents are extremely concerned about his weight, so they continue with the pureed foods and liquid supplements.

The fear and stress experienced by Dillon's parents is very real and should be recognized by the professionals working with the family. Unfortunately, the longer the parents support Dillon's rigid food selections, the more difficult it will be to broaden his food choices in the future. Parents of children with disabilities must find a balance between their personal beliefs about the disability and their long term goal of normal eating behaviors.

***An Exercise in Eating***

In order to acknowledge the grieving process and move forward with a treatment plan, parents and professionals should examine their past.

- Write down three judgments you hold about the child. For example, "this child deliberately won't eat" or "this child is a bad eater"
- Replace those judgments with new and more positive strengths about the child. For example, "this child is learning to eat new foods"
- Share your written thoughts with the other members of the team
- Verbally acknowledge those feelings to the child

By going through the process of acceptance and changing one's beliefs, parents and professionals can begin to move forward with a new vision of the child.

## Conclusion

While the main focus of this chapter is on assisting parents and professionals in determining some of the causes of eating challenges, team members themselves are encouraged to let go of any preconceived negative judgments of the child. In the past, a resistant eater was often judged as "bad" or noncompliant at the dinner table. Indeed, many people view a resistant eater as being deliberately stubborn or spoiled. These negative labels may distort our views of all future possibilities for the child. The purpose of reviewing the cause(s) is to assist the team in designing a plan based on a clear understanding of the child's strengths and areas needed for learning new skills.

Whatever the initial environmental and behavioral causes are for a resistant eater, it is important for families to begin to understand that they can work with their child to change the future. Although the situation for the child and parent may appear grim at the moment, it is not too late to provide a new mealtime environment and support the child in experiencing new foods. Resistant eaters of all ages can begin a treatment plan and learn new skills to experience new foods. Parents may feel guilt or shame over their past efforts to coerce their children to eat, but children are forgiving. If parents begin to let go of their cultural roadblocks about eating and beliefs about their child, the family can begin to heal and the child will feel safe and secure to explore new foods.

Several environmental and behavioral factors should be reviewed when determining the exact nature of problem eating. Some children may require further assessment. Sensory integration dysfunction and oral-motor delays should also be assessed by an appropriate multidisciplinary evaluation team. In the next chapter we will take a closer look at the effects of sensory and motor problems on eating.

# CHAPTER FOUR

# Sensory-Based and Motor-Based Problems Affecting the Resistant Eater

Chapter Two provided a summary of the stages the typical child goes through in oral-motor development. This included the positions the child usually assumes while feeding and motor development as it pertains to feeding skills. In this chapter we will define sensory integration and discuss how sensory integration dysfunction (SID) affects the resistant eater. The latter part of the chapter will highlight the need to determine whether the resistant eater's difficulties are motor- or sensory-based. Some red flags or indicators are provided to assist the reader in determining whether the child demonstrates oral-motor dysfunction and describe how the sensory issues or motor issues affect the child's skills. The chapter will also briefly describe the body's sensory systems and how they can affect performance during mealtimes.

## Sensory Integration Dysfunction

A. Jean Ayres, Ph.D., an occupational therapist, developed the theory of sensory integration in the 1950s and 1960s. Our central nervous system (our brain and spinal cord) has the ability to take in the many sensations we receive from our bodies and from the world around us.

Our sensory system consists of:

- Proprioception (body awareness)
- Vestibular (balance)
- Tactile (touch)
- Gustatory (taste)
- Olfactory (smell)
- Vision
- Auditory (hearing)

Our brain receives information from the sensory systems listed above, interprets the information, and organizes our purposeful response. In this way, we are able to learn and function smoothly in activities of daily life because we have adequate sensory integration skills.

Sensory integration dysfunction occurs when the brain cannot efficiently process the sensory information coming from the body or from the environment. Therefore, causing the person with sensory integration dysfunction to experience difficulties responding in an adaptive way to everyday sensations that other people hardly notice.

This chapter provides an overview of the different sensory systems, defining their functional importance as it pertains to mealtime experiences.

**Proprioceptive Sensory Information**

Proprioception relates to the sensations we receive from our tendons, muscles, and joints. The proprioceptive system gives us information about joint position and movement.

The child with poor proprioception experiences difficulties interpreting sensations regarding the position and movement of her head and limbs. The child has a poor sense of body awareness, not having a mental picture of her own body parts and where they are in relation to each other. Motor planning is very difficult because she is unable to control and monitor her gross motor and fine motor muscles.

Ineffective processing of proprioceptive information can affect the resistant eater's mealtime participation and feeding skills in the following areas:

- Child may have a problem with adjusting or grading the amount of jaw opening needed to bite foods of different thicknesses and in grading the power or force of the bite for chewing.
- Child may hold and use eating utensils with too much or too little force.
- Child may slump in the chair, unable to maintain an upright position.
- Child may have difficulty knowing where her body is in relation to objects and people, frequently bumping into obstacles, knocking a glass of juice over, dropping utensils, or falling off the chair.
- Child may not know how much pressure to exert when flexing and extending her muscles, spilling juice all over her face when she brings the cup to her mouth, or spilling soups and cereal when she scoops it with her spoon.

***Colton***

Colton experiences difficulties drinking from a cup. His mother reports that he constantly asks to use a straw because it's easier. When there isn't a straw available, Colton tends to get the liquid all over himself instead of into his mouth. His mother notes that it is as if Colton does not know when to stop tilting the cup. During his occupational therapy session, it was determined that Colton exhibited poor registration of proprioceptive information. This affects his drinking skills in the following ways:

- He is unable to adjust the speed at which his arms move and he is unable to perform a smooth, coordinated movement of tilting the cup upwards.
- The liquid may be moving so quickly that Colton is not getting sufficient sensory-weight feedback to allow the tongue to adjust its configuration to collect the liquid more efficiently.

Colton's drinking skills improved when:

- He used a cup with a weighted base—this provided more proprioceptive information to his arm and hand.
- He drank a heavier liquid, such as a fruit smoothie, milkshake or a mixture of juice and applesauce. The heavier liquid gave Colton enough proprioceptive feedback to start a smooth suck-swallow drinking response.

***Kerry***

Kerry had a hard time focusing on the mealtime process—her attention seemed diverted to extraneous arm, head, and foot movements. When Kerry was seated in a beanbag chair (providing deep pressure at the shoulder and hip joints), it helped to increase her awareness of her body in space. As her awareness increased, the extraneous movements reduced. In this way, proprioceptive information provided a calming effect for Kerry allowing her to focus on the mealtime.

**Vestibular Sensory Information**

The vestibular system gives us information about the position of our heads and bodies in relation to the surface of the earth. This system:

- Takes in sensory messages about balance and movement from the neck, eyes, and body
- Sends these messages to the central nervous system for processing
- Helps generate muscle tone that allows us to move smoothly and efficiently

The vestibular system, in combination with the proprioceptive and visual systems, tells us whether we are moving or standing still, and whether objects are moving or motionless in relation to our body. It also informs us about which direction we are going and whether we are speeding up or slowing down. Controlled movements such as rolling, crawling, moving through space, sitting still, standing, running, and performing sport skills all rely on the vestibular system giving the appropriate information to our nervous systems.

The vestibular system has yet another important function—it influences the pre-arousal part of the brain. This is the part of the brain that controls alertness and the ability to focus. Depending on the type of vestibular stimulation, the influence can alert (wake up) or calm a child's nervous system. Have you noticed that when a child is struggling to stay awake, he tends to stay active by running around? When you are driving for many hours and start to feel sleepy, doesn't it wake you up when you stop the car and walk around for a little while? Movement that is slow, predictable, even, or rhythmic, and particularly movements in a straight line, has a calming effect on the nervous system of children. Often the slow motion of a car moving in a straight line has a magic effect on many fussy children—it calms them down or lulls them asleep.

Ineffective processing of vestibular information can affect the resistant eater's mealtime participation and feeding skills in the following areas:

- The child may focus all her attention on how she is moving or the fact that she is not moving.
- The child may be constantly alerted to her body's position in space, for example if the child is leaning to one side, she may be overly focused on her body's position and her fear of falling. This prevents her from concentrating on the eating experience.

The child needs to focus on the meal, the food, the eating process, and the mealtime interactions. Direct attention to vestibular information can distract from the meal.

***Max***

Max has low muscle tone. When you try to lift him, he is not able to help you. He feels heavier than his actual weight. The parts of his body that you are not supporting just flop toward the ground. When Max pays attention to eating his food, his body looks like it has melted onto his chair like hot wax. He leans against the backrest or the table to support his body. His parents never dare give him a stool to sit on because he constantly falls off of it.

Vestibular input can create changes in muscle tone. This contributes to how the body constantly adjusts to the pull of gravity. As in Max's case, low muscle tone can cause a child to be unable to control himself against the downward pull of gravity.

Some children do not have enough tonic muscle control or strength to hold a body part steady. They rely on phasic muscle control—they repeatedly contract and relax groups of muscles in phases. If you ask a child with poor muscle tone to hold her arms outstretched for a few minutes, her arms will constantly bounce up and down. A child with poor muscle control will be unable to sit still, for example, during mealtimes, because her body has to be in constant motion. It is required during mealtimes that the body remain steady so that the arm and hand can reach for the fork, stab the food, then bring the food up to the mouth. If the whole body follows the arm, the child may fall over or the excess motion may interfere with smooth and safe control of the fork.

If children with vestibular problems concentrate on sitting still, they are able to consciously contract their muscles to hold still. However, the minute they are asked to do another task, their concentration shifts to the new task.

***Joseph and Mike***

During a field trip to a park, the class is sitting in a circle on the grass to share a picnic lunch. Joseph, who has low muscle tone, cannot remain sitting upright and before long is observed to start gradually leaning on his arms, then his elbows, and eventually he is lying on his side or stomach. Mike, on the other hand, cannot sit still. He sits on his knees, changes to a squat, then starts pushing down on his hands so his feet are suspended in the air, and before long, Mike is standing up and jumping while trying to eat his sandwich and talk to his friends.

It is important to consider the child's muscle tone and motor-planning abilities when developing a mealtime program. If muscle tension is too tight or too loose or fluctuates rapidly, the child can become frustrated because it is difficult to perform the desired movements, as attention is focused on how difficult it is to move. When the child sits unsteadily in the chair with his head and body tilted to one side and feet dangling, the vestibular system demands attention and the child is less able to focus on the more important eating and social aspects of the meal. A child who is positioned in any vestibularly alerting posture must primarily attend to the vestibular input and only secondarily attend to the meal.

When the vestibular system inefficiently processes movement sensations, the child may:

- Overreact or be hypersensitive to movement, or
- Seek a lot of movement sensations, be hyposensitive

The child who is hypersensitive or overreacts to vestibular sensory information would benefit from being positioned in a stable, well-supported position during mealtimes. In most cases, it would be a stationary, comfortable position in a chair with feet touching the floor or a stable surface.

| **Table 4.1** ***Characteristics of a Child Overreacting to Vestibular Sensations*** |
|---|
| • Dislikes playground activities, such as swinging, spinning, and sliding<br>• Unusually cautious, slow-moving and sedentary, hesitating to take risks<br>• Becomes car sick/motion sick<br>• Easily loses his balance when climbing stairs, riding a bicycle, hopping, walking on a balance beam, or standing on one foot<br>• Moves in an uncoordinated, awkward way<br>• Has a fear of falling, even where no real danger exists, for example sitting in a beanbag chair or car seat<br>• Is fearful of heights, even slightly raised surfaces such as curbs, steps, mats<br>• Becomes anxious when his feet leave the ground |

During mealtimes, children who are hyposensitive to vestibular sensations as described in table 4.2 might benefit from sitting on surfaces that allow more movement such as a ball, a T-stool or a "Move 'N' Sit" cushion. Children who seek extra vestibular input might need frequent breaks from the table so that they can stand up and move around before going back to sitting. Often, these children will benefit from being allowed to swing, run or play vigorously prior to their mealtimes.

| **Table 4.2** *Characteristics of Hyposensitivity to Vestibular Sensations* |
| --- |
| • Need to keep moving as much as possible in order to function; have trouble sitting still or staying in their seat<br>• Repeatedly and vigorously shake their head, rock back and forth, jump up and down<br>• Crave intense movement experiences, such as bouncing on furniture, or assuming upside-down positions<br>• Do not get dizzy even after twirling in circles or spinning rapidly for a lengthy period<br>• Enjoy swinging very high and for long periods of time<br>• Are fidgety and clumsy<br>• Have a loose and floppy body<br>• Tend to slump in their chair or sprawl over the table, prefer to lie down rather than sit upright<br>• Constantly lean their head on their arms or hands |

Vestibular input can alert or calm a child. Fast movement such as bouncing, running, or swinging high can alert the vestibular system. Slow movement such as rocking or swaying side to side can have a calming effect on the vestibular system. Each child's vestibular system has different needs and should be considered individually. Based on these needs, determine if you need to alert or calm the child's vestibular system before or during a meal. Make appropriate adjustments to maximize the mealtime experience.

***Emil***

Emil's teacher calls him a "wet noodle." He never seems to hold himself upright and tends to lie on the table half way through the snack time. It is also difficult to get Emil to pay attention to the meal. He does not look at his food. During mealtimes, Emil receives a "Move 'N' Sit" cushion or a ball to sit on. This provides him with the opportunity to move and receive alerting vestibular input while staying at the table. Emil is now able to remain at the table in an upright, seated position for the duration of a snack and to pay more attention to feeding himself.

Sometimes vestibular stimulation, in the form of gentle movement, during a meal can help a child become more organized for the meal. Another child might require more alerting vestibular stimulation during mealtimes. This might be done by placing the child on a ball so that he can gently bounce between bites of food. However vestibular sensory information is used, the focus should be on promoting postural control and the attention needs of the child to enable eating and participating in mealtime routines.

**Tactile Sensory Information**

The tactile system is one of the first sensory systems to develop, functioning in the fetus as early as seven and a half weeks after conception. The mouth, lips, tongue, fingers, and hands are the most sensitive to touch. During the prenatal period and the first few months of the child's life, the mouth is one of the few ways in which infants gain information about their world. This is one of the reasons why infants and toddlers put everything they touch in their mouths.

For each area of the body that is touched, there is a specific area in the sensory cortex of the brain where the stimulation is recorded and a map of the skin surface is created. This is how the child knows where he has been touched. The fingers, thumbs, and lips are the most sensitive parts of the body. Spaces in the sensory cortex of the brain created by impulses from these sensitive areas are larger than all the space reserved for impulses from all the other parts of the body.

Tactile dysfunction occurs when the tactile system fails to register the information (hyposensitive) from the tactile receptors or reacts defensively to the tactile information (hypersensitive).

Have you ever been tricked into shaking someone's hand and he has a buzzer hidden in his palm? That tactile stimulus would have probably alarmed you or made you angry, even though it was not painful. Your reaction would have been less if you had known that the person had the buzzer in his hand. Quick, unexpected, or light touch sensations tend to alert the nervous system more than firm, non-moving pressure sensations.

**Table 4.3** ***Symptoms of Children Who are Under Responsive or Hyposensitive to Touch Sensations***

- Seem unaware of touch unless it is very intense
- Unaware of messiness on their face, especially around the mouth and nose, do not notice crumbs on their face or a runny nose
- Show little or no reaction to pain from scrapes, bruises, cuts or shots
- Fail to realize that they have dropped something
- Seem out of touch with their hands, as if they are unfamiliar appendages
- Unable to identify body parts that have been touched without looking
- Difficulty holding and using tools such as spoons, forks, crayons, scissors
- Seek certain messy experiences (play dough, finger painting, shaving foam) often for long periods of time
- Rub or even bite their own skin repeatedly
- Use their mouth to investigate objects even after the age of two

To the tactilely defensive child a simple touch on the arm or leg may be perceived as a primal threat causing the child to react negatively such as becoming angry, fighting or running away. The following table describes the characteristics of a child who overreacts to tactile sensations.

| Table 4.4 | *Children Who are Oversensitive to Touch Stimuli or Tactile Defensive* |
|---|---|

- Dislike messy activities such as play dough, using glue or finger painting
- Are bothered by certain types of clothing for example wool or coarse fabrics
- Prefer food to be the same temperature
- Avoid lumpy foods or foods with different textures (i.e. chunky peanut butter, rice, vegetables)
- Become aggressive or anxious on windy days
- Dislike having hair cut or toenails cut
- Dislike having their teeth brushed
- Dislike swimming or bathing

***Austin***

Austin is an example of how tactile defensiveness can affect a child's social eating skills. Austin hates to go to birthday parties. During the summer months the parties usually involve swimming. Austin dislikes wearing a bathing suit because he dislikes having his skin exposed, the water is always too cold to touch, and he hates anything wet touching him, especially if it touches his face. Austin will scream and get upset when his friends splash in the pool and accidentally spray him. He prefers to play on his own, away from the pool and the wet children. When it is time to eat the birthday cake, Austin usually refuses a piece of cake because he can't stand to get any frosting on his face. As a result, Austin's classmates have stopped inviting him to their birthday parties.

The texture in foods may cause the child with gustatory sensitivities discomfort and may lead to food refusal. Foods can be hard or soft, wet or dry, lumpy or smooth. Foods differ in shapes and size. Some foods such as pretzels are crunchy and others are chewy (Twizzlers). There are so many combinations and contrasts in food texture. Some children make the texture transitions easily and with enthusiasm. Children with hypersensitivity to textured foods may need to make these transitions slowly and in tiny increments.

Touch draws attention to or away from an activity. Used prescriptively, touch can prepare a child for a meal and help focus attention on the desired interaction. For example, Austin's tactile sensitivity around his mouth decreased after he received sensory integration therapy. Some of the tactile activities his treatment plan included were: allowing him to wipe his face with different textured washcloths; applying deep pressure strokes to his lips and cheeks; wiping his face with a lukewarm washcloth before meals and playing with fans blowing on his face. The following table 4.5 defines alerting or calming touch sensations.

### Gustatory Sensory Information (Taste)

The taste buds of the tongue receive and interpret gustatory sensory information. They interpret sweet, sour, bitter, and salty. Taste can also differ by being strong, or weak, concentrated or diluted. A child who is sensitive to tastes and changes may find it easier to accept food with milder, dilute tastes. For example, a taste-sensitive child may find it difficult to transition from water to juice.

| Table 4.5 *Alerting Touch Sensations and Calming Touch Sensations* | |
|---|---|
| **Alerting touch sensations**<br>• Uneven or rough textures (i.e. wool, raw silk, burlap)<br>• The extremes of hot and cold<br>• Light ticklish touch<br>• Vibration (i.e. an electric toothbrush) | **Calming touch sensations**<br>• Smooth, even textures (i.e. satin, percale cotton, velvet)<br>• Neutral, warm temperatures<br>• Deep-pressure touch (i.e. firmly wrapped in a soft weighted blanket, wearing a weighted vest, sitting in a beanbag chair)<br>Deep pressure is initially noticeable or alerting, but when it is continued, it becomes calming or quieting sensory input as the person gets used to the touch |

The gustatory system works in close contact with the olfactory system (smell) to finely interpret taste. That's why a bad cold usually decreases the appetite and food that has no smell tastes bland.

An important fact to remember when an adult is preparing food for a child to eat is that children often respond differently to taste than adults. Adults often require stronger-flavored foods to build awareness because they lose taste buds as they age. Studies have found that certain medical conditions, medications, and even a mild deficiency of zinc can cause distortions in taste and cause the child to refuse food.

| **Table 4.6** *Decreased Taste Sensitivity vs. Increased Taste Sensitivity* | |
|---|---|
| **A child with decreased taste sensitivity may:**<br>• Lick or taste inedible objects, such as play dough and toys<br>• Prefer very hot or spicy foods<br>• Prefer very hot or cold foods | **A child with increased taste sensitivity may:**<br>• Object to certain textures of food (i.e. lumpy, mashed or chewy foods)<br>• Object to certain temperatures of food (i.e. very hot, lukewarm, ice cold)<br>• Gag often when eating |

Changing the taste sensation of the child's food may improve the child's ability to integrate the sensory information in more effective and appropriate ways. For example, children who are poorly alerted to food or are unmotivated to eat may respond and eat better when herbs and spices are added. In contrast, children experiencing difficulty organizing and integrating sensory information may be more accepting of food when less alerting foods, such as those with sour or bitter tastes, are eliminated from the diet. Often parents and professionals fall into the trap of introducing more sweet flavored foods into the child's diet because they accept it more readily. Do not predominantly use sweet-tasting foods because it is easy for people to become addicted to sweets.

### Olfactory Sensory Information (Smell)

Smell perception occurs when the chemicals stimulate the olfactory receptors in the nasal cavity. As mentioned, smell and taste are intertwined. In fact, about 75% of taste perceptions depend on an efficient sense of smell. Some children are able to interpret flavor information more strongly with a stronger sense of smell. Others with chronic congestion or who constantly breathe through their mouth, cannot interpret the flavor of food effectively.

Flavor perception, therefore, requires a combination of the olfactory and gustatory systems. As proof, most people recall their response to food when they have a cold, remembering how nose congestion interfered with the ability to taste foods. Food flavors needed to be quite strong to be tasted. Parents and professionals need to consider this factor when working with children who are chronically congested with a stuffy nose. These children are losing not only smell but also taste information. They have little desire to eat the foods presented to them. Food choices for these children are extremely important. Stronger or spicier flavors may make the difference in peaking the child's interest level, motivation to eat and appreciation of the meal.

Smells are picked up in the nasal cavity and interpreted in the brain. When we smell something, the olfactory stimulus goes directly to the limbic system. The limbic system is the section of the brain that is primarily involved with one's emotions and inner drive. For this reason, smell has a strong emotional component and a strong association with memory storage. Smells are very memorable!

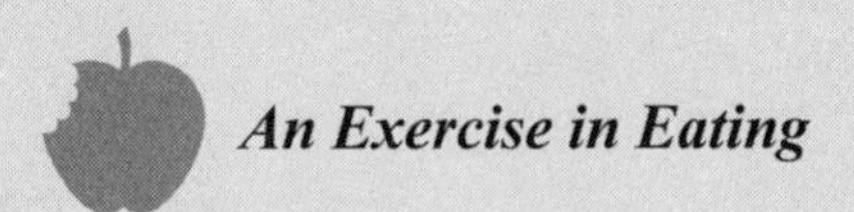

*An Exercise in Eating*

Have you ever smelled a fragrance or odor and immediately remembered a time and place when you previously experienced that smell? The smell of jasmine always reminds me of lazing around the swimming pool at our home in South Africa. On the wall surrounding the pool grew the most beautiful, sweet-smelling jasmine.

Think of an odor that reminds you of a childhood memory.

What does the smell of fresh bread remind you of?

How do you feel when you smell cooked cabbage?

Smells may also have unpleasant connotations. A child may remember an uncomfortable experience with a particular food or with a smell in the environment (such as fresh paint or the smell of an adult's deodorant), and that negative memory may be contributing to her current difficulty in accepting or handling that specific food. For this reason, one needs to investigate if there are other strong smells in the environment competing with the food smells.

For many reasons, smell is an important part of the meal. For example, the smell of the food usually is a child's first hint that the meal is forthcoming. In a classroom setting where many children eat at one time, diaper odors or the smell of a disinfectant can compete with the smell of food, making it difficult for the child to attend to the meal. For older children eating in the cafeteria, the odor of fried food may put a child off of eating.

| Table 4.7 | *Characteristics of Children with Olfactory Dysfunction* |
|---|---|

- Oversensitive to smells
- Object to odors that other children do not notice
- Undersensitive to odors
- Ignore unpleasant odors

***Isobel***

Isobel's mother could never place a bowl of fruit salad on the table during meals without causing Isobel to start fussing and complaining and eventually refusing to eat. Faced with any unfamiliar or unpleasant smell (which encompassed many foods outside her limited diet), Isobel would say that it smelled like "dead chicken." The result was that Isobel's family would eat their food in the kitchen, before sitting down to watch Isobel eat her food. The family avoided any holiday get-togethers at friends' houses because Isobel would disrupt the meal to the extent that she would have to be carried away from the table kicking and screaming.

**Visual Sensory Information**

The eyes work together to give visual information. They focus on objects near and far, track in vertical, horizontal, diagonal, and circular directions; and can converge and diverge focus. People have central (front) vision as well as peripheral (side) vision.

Visual dysfunction is experienced when the brain is unable to link visual information with auditory, touch and movement sensations or it inadequately processes the sensory messages. For example, inefficient processing of the visual and auditory system will result in the child not knowing where to look when the teacher calls his name; inefficient processing of the visual and tactile system will result in the child's inability to know—just by looking—that a glass of water is heavier than an empty plastic cup; inefficient processing of sight with movement will cause a child to trip over uneven surfaces or bump into objects. Therefore, a child with visual dysfunction may have difficulties with eye-hand coordination, visual perception, and spatial awareness.

How the child with a visual dysfunction may experience difficulties at mealtimes:

- Shield her eyes to screen out sights
- Cover one eye or squint when focusing on objects that are close
- Have difficulty shifting her gaze from one object to another
- Have difficulty with fine-motor tasks involving spatial relationships for example, overreaching for the fork/spoon or being unable to scoop cereal onto the spoon
- Misjudge spatial relationships of objects in the environment, often bumping into furniture
- Be uncomfortable or overwhelmed by moving objects or people
- Fatigue easily
- Withdraw from group participation—visually too overwhelming

| Table 4.8 *Alerting Visual Stimuli Sensations and Calming Visual Stimuli* | |
|---|---|
| **Alerting visual stimuli sensations** | **Calming visual stimuli** |
| • Brighter primary colors<br>• Shiny objects (i.e. chrome, mirrors)<br>• Moving objects (i.e. fans, flags, advertising displays), especially if the movement is unexpected<br>• Peripheral movements<br>• Contrasts in color, shape, or movement (i.e. yellow and black stripes) | • Pale, neutral colors<br>• Objects with a dull finish<br>• Familiar pictures<br>• Stationary objects<br>• Movements occurring in the center of vision<br>• Blends of color and form |

Occasionally, children who are described as distractible, hyperactive, or indifferent to foods and objects respond in these ways because of a visual field deficit. That is, they fail at times to respond because food or an object is presented in a field in which they have no vision. At other times they respond appropriately because the object is within a quadrant where there is usable vision. Be sure to determine the child's optimum field of vision by consulting with the child's ophthalmologist, optometrist or functional vision specialist, if necessary.

### Auditory Sensory Information (Hearing)

Sound is transmitted as sound waves, touching the eardrum, causing the eardrum to vibrate. When hearing is intact, a person can localize the direction of a sound and discriminate between a wide variety of environmental and speech sounds.

Loud, intermittent, unexpected and high-pitched sounds tend to get a person's attention more rapidly. On the other hand, soft, repetitive, familiar, sustained, and low-pitched sounds may be ignored. People often quiet their behavior when these sounds are in the background. Basic characteristics of music influence the functioning of the body (Campbell, 1997). Music with a slow tempo and a regular, sustained rhythm slows down breathing and heart rhythms, contributing to greater relaxation.

***Sven***

Sven has just started first grade. His mother couldn't understand why he would come home every day with a full lunchbox. He hardly touched any of his food. She knew he was hungry at that time because he had always eaten his lunch in kindergarten. After visiting his school, she realized that he didn't have lunch in his classroom anymore. Sven and the rest of his class sat at a table in the school's multipurpose room together with all the other classes in the school. Sven was observed to sit the entire lunchtime with his hands over his ears. The noise was simply too much for him to endure.

Children can ignore intense visual stimulation by shutting their eyes or looking away from the meal or the feeder. But auditory stimulation is always there; it cannot be ignored. Some children attempt to deal with the overload and confusion by engaging in rhythmical stereotyped movements such as flapping the hands or rocking.

| Table 4.9 *Characteristics of Children with Auditory Dysfunction* |
|---|
| • Overly distressed and anxious by noises that are loud, sudden or high-pitched (i.e. fire alarm, smoke alarm), or by sounds that do not usually bother others (i.e. chairs scraping on the floor)<br>• Have trouble attending to verbal instructions<br>• Unable to follow multi-step verbal instructions<br>• Unable to attend to one voice or sound without being distracted by other sounds<br>• Have trouble identifying voices or discriminating between sounds<br>• Unaware of the source of sounds, and may look all around to locate where the sounds come from |

Distracting sounds should be eliminated or reduced from the mealtime area whenever possible. Once the overall noise level is reduced, sound can be used directly to quiet the child and focus attention.

A number of research studies have addressed the effect of background music on mealtime behaviors. During sessions in which soothing background music was played, patients ate more food, were calmer, and had reductions in agitation, anxiety, fear, and depression during the meal. They spent more time at the dinner table and ate more calmly.

**Modulation**

Our brain is equipped to modulate sensory messages in order to respond appropriately and automatically to them. *Modulation* describes the process the brain uses to regulate the bodies' activities. Our mental, physical, and emotional activity levels are dependent on this process of modulation. Modulation balances the flow of sensory information coming into the central nervous system.

We are constantly receiving a multitude of sensations. Most of these sensations are irrelevant to our situation and therefore the brain inhibits them. Without inhibition, we would be paying attention to every sensation—useful or not. When we meet a good friend for dinner in a restaurant, our bodies are taking in sensations of how the chair feels, the height of the table, the feel of the napkin on our lap, and the background noise (music playing or other conversations going on). We are able to inhibit these sensations so we can focus on conversing with our friend and enjoying our food.

Facilitation is the neurological process that promotes connections between sensory intake and behavioral output. When we are doing something meaningful and beneficial, our brain tells us to stay alert and pay attention. For example, when you start to feel tired on a long drive, you might turn up the radio, drink something cold, chew gum or stop the car and walk around to wake up.

When inhibition and facilitation are balanced, we can make smooth transitions in our physical, mental and emotional state. Therefore, we can switch gears from inattention to attention, from drowsiness to alertness, from sulks to smiles and from relaxation to readiness for action.

The following are examples of how modulation affects a child's behavior:

***Susan***

*A child with normal sensory integration skills:* It's lunchtime and the children are walking in a line to the multipurpose room. Susan is able to carry her lunch tin while negotiating her way across the school's courtyard, stepping over the curb that separates the grass from the pavement. Her classmate behind her isn't paying attention, when Susan stops at the door, and bumps into her. Susan turns around and smiles when her friend apologizes. She gets to her seat, is able to open her lunch container and enjoy the food her mother prepared that day. After lunch, she plays tag with a group of children before going back to class and is attentive to the afternoon activities.

***Raquel***

*A child with sensory integration dysfunction:* Raquel has tripped a few times on the way to the multipurpose room. She dropped her lunch tin when she stumbled over the curb, and when the girl behind her bumps into her, she explodes and screams, "Don't touch me!" She struggles to open her lunch container, spilling the juice from the juice box because she squeezes it too hard. Complaining that the noise is too loud in the room, she doesn't eat much of her lunch. After lunch, she spends her time wiping the juice off her shirt, crying that the wetness is uncomfortable. She returns to class and is unable to calm down and attend to the reading lesson.

The more effective our brain is at processing the sensory information we take in (sensory intake), the more effective our behavioral response (motor output) is. Further, the more effective our response, the more feedback we receive to help us take in new sensory information and continue the never-ending process of sensory integration.

## How to Use and Organize the Information We Have About the Resistant Eater

Once sufficient observation has been made of the child's oral-motor skills as well as what effect various sensory input has on the child's performance during eating and non-eating activities it is necessary to organize the information and determine appropriate intervention strategies.

***Chandler***

In *Pre-Feeding Skills: A Comprehensive Resource for Mealtime Development, 2nd ed.* (2000), Suzanne Evans Morris and Marsha Dunn Klein describe a scenario, which has been played out so often despite professional's best intentions. "Many therapists create treatment recommendations and programs that work on individual splinter skills. Often these splinter skills are inappropriate for the child because the child needs prerequisite skills. For example, one therapist developed a program around the treatment goal to teach 5-year-old Chandler to chew. She worked diligently with recommendations and techniques to obtain tongue lateralization (moving tongue side to side). She placed food between the lateral biting surfaces of the teeth as Chandler's tongue moved in and out of his mouth, and he would grimace and complain. Another therapist showed her how

***Chandler cont.***

to stimulate the sides of the tongue with a Nuk Massage brush, and Chandler began to cry. She developed a program to reinforce his positive attempts to move his tongue and to punish his complaining and crying. Chandler hated coming to therapy, but still the therapist persisted in her goals to help him develop chewing skills. The therapist was correct in identifying Chandler's lack of chewing skills. However, she did not associate his strong suckle pattern of the tongue and his oral sensory defensiveness with his lack of chewing. Chandler hated any stimulation in his mouth. He had never put his fingers in his mouth and had never mouthed or explored toys. He barely accepted the feeling of pureed food on the spoon. If she had spent their time helping him develop a comfortable relationship with non-food sensory input in the mouth, he would have developed many of the separate skills that depend on this foundational skill. She would also have avoided developing the stressful adversarial relationship that evolved. The most important thing that Chandler learned was to hate therapy and be extremely cautious and suspicious about anyone who approached his mouth." (p 187.)

CHAPTER FIVE

# Motor-Based Eating Problems

# vs.

# Sensory-Based Eating Problems

Resistant eaters with *motor-based eating problems* show difficulties in muscle tone and movement patterns. They may have low, high, or fluctuating muscle tone and have difficulty coordinating and timing mouth and body movements. This also affects the coordination of their sucking, swallowing, and breathing.

***Miguel***

Miguel has mild low tone and poor postural control. He enjoys sucking on any of the foods presented to him during snack time. He has difficulty chewing because of his low tone. For example, he is unable to bite through a cracker, let alone meat and other chewy foods. Although he can move his tongue to the side when food is placed between his teeth, he has difficulty keeping the tongue in place while he chews. As a result, food falls into the cheek cavity (between cheek and teeth) or onto the back of his tongue before he has finished chewing. He sometimes gags or chokes because he is unable to physically control the movement of the solid food. Miguel is a child with a motor-based eating problem.

Low muscle tone (hypotonia) in the tongue reduces strength and skill for effective and safe eating. When the tone is low, the child's tongue appears thick and rounded. It needs to be thin, cupped or have a grooved configuration for effective sucking.

Many children with low tone in the tongue dislike eating foods, such as meats, that require longer, more sustained chewing. Due to the child's decreased skill in organizing the food in the mouth and directing it to the pharynx for swallowing, food and liquid may fall over the tongue into the space between the cheek and the teeth or fall out of the mouth.

In brief, low muscle tone in the tongue: (a) affects the quality of the child's eating skills (b) compromises the quantity that the child consumes (because the child fatigues more easily), and (c) can negatively impact speech production.

Low muscle tone in the cheeks is common. Often, children with low tone in their face experience difficulties with facial movement and facial expression. As a result, they give the impression that they do not understand what others are saying or that they are cognitively delayed. Low tone in the cheeks may cause the child's mouth to hang open and excessive drooling may occur.

***Maria***

Maria demonstrates hypersensitivity to sounds and unexpected noises and she avoids being touched. Her feeding problems began when her mother introduced pureed foods. She did not like the spoon in her mouth and she spat the food out. At the sight of food, Maria starts to gag. Maria is a child with a sensory-based eating problem.

Resistant eaters with *sensory-based feeding problems* experience difficulty eating because their sensory systems do not support the eating and drinking process. For example, their sensory systems may overreact to certain food textures and odors. They may overreact or underreact to oral sensory information or to their environment. They may be highly distractible or have strong emotional reactions when something happens that they perceive as a threat or as uncomfortable. They may experience sensory overload at mealtimes.

Sensory and motor limitations contribute significantly to the presence of food aversions. Children with special needs are often given foods that they don't have the motor skills to handle or foods that do not address their sensory deficits. As a result, children will respond by gagging, choking or throwing up. The subsequent learned reaction is that food can be harmful or even perceived as painful, therefore it is better to just avoid it all costs.

**Reflux and Other Gastrointestinal Problems**

Another reason for children to resist eating is the fact that they may be experiencing gastrointestinal discomfort. The gastrointestinal (GI) system influences the child's desire to eat and the way the child eats. For many children with feeding problems, the GI system may not be working well and as a result may negatively influence their desire to eat as well as their appetite and growth.

The child who is experiencing gastrointestinal problems find eating to be unpleasant and unsafe. To protect himself from experiencing discomfort and pain, the child can become very picky about what he eats and his appetite may become suppressed. It is important to understand the relationship between gastrointestinal symptoms and feeding, appetite and growth. The most carefully planned feeding programs, oral-motor techniques, and positioning changes will not be successful until the GI symptoms (nausea, gagging, retching, vomiting, pain, etc. are addressed. A child's feeding issues can worsen if gastrointestinal discomfort is not understood and treated properly.

Gastroesophageal Reflux (GER) occurs when the stomach's acidic contents move backward into the esophagus. If the lower esophageal sphincter (the muscle connecting the esophagus with the stomach) relaxes or is weak, it can allow the stomach contents to reflux.

Signs and symptoms may include:

- Heartburn is the most common symptom in children and adults. It is worse after meals and can last up to 2 hours. Children experiencing reflux may feel like the food is coming back up into the mouth, leaving a bitter aftertaste of stomach acid. The symptoms may worsen if the child lies down after a meal.
- Nausea

- Arching or stiffening of the body in response to swallowing
- Frequent swallowing with facial grimaces
- Pain, irritability, or constant or sudden crying after eating
- Frequent coughs, hiccups
- Frequent spitting up or vomiting after eating
- Vomiting more than 1 hour after eating
- Regular spitting up that continues after the first year
- Inability to sleep soundly
- “Wet burp” or “wet hiccup” sounds
- Poor weight gain or weight loss
- Constant eating and drinking
- Inability to eat certain foods
- Refusing food or accepting only a few bites despite hunger
- Swallowing problems (such as gagging or choking)
- Hoarse voice
- Frequent sore throats
- Frequent respiratory problems (such as pneumonia, bronchitis, wheezing, or coughing)
- Bad breath
- Drooling

Because of constant reflux of stomach acid, the esophagus can become red and irritated (esophagitis). Constant refluxing is painful and can cause a child to refuse to eat. If severe, GER can cause bleeding and scar tissue, which can cause the child to experience difficulties with swallowing. The child loses nutrients from spitting up. Since the child often has a decreased desire to eat, proper nutrition is a concern. Respiratory problems are another possible complication as the stomach contents may enter the windpipe, lungs, or nose and as a result, the child can develop breathing problems, sinus congestion or pneumonia.

For extensive information on diagnosing and treating gastrointestinal discomfort, the reader is referred to Chapters Twenty-Two and Twenty-Three in *Pre-Feeding Skills: A Comprehensive Resource for Mealtime Development, 2nd ed.* (2000) written by Suzanne Evans Morris and Marsha Dunn Klein.

The rest of this chapter will:

- Review possible indicators (red flags) of oral-motor dysfunction
- Provide a brief description of the motor-based and sensory-based factors that may be contributing to the dysfunction

If the child is observed to demonstrate any of the following signs, there is a possibility that the child has oral-motor dysfunction.

Indicators of oral-motor dysfunction:

- Abnormal sucking pattern
- Nasal reflux

- Aspiration
- Gagging
- Drooling
- Tooth grinding
- Limited upper-lip movement
- Immature spoon feeding skills
- Immature cup drinking skills
- Immature biting skills

We will address each of these indicators in more detail. Please keep in mind that this book by no means covers all aspects of oral-motor dysfunction. When the reader determines, based on the knowledge gained in this book, that oral-motor difficulties are present in a child that are compromising the child's feeding abilities and contributing to the child being a resistant eater, the reader should seek a professional assessment from an occupational therapist or speech and language pathologist who specializes in feeding difficulties and oral-motor treatment.

**Abnormal Sucking Pattern**

During sucking, the child experiencing difficulties with timing and coordinating the suck-swallow-breath sequence often coughs, chokes or splutters.

With a child who experiences sensory dysfunction, oral sucking movements may become disorganized when the tongue is touched. If the environment is too stimulating (such as loud noises, bright lights, too many people), the infant may react by becoming disorganized in his behavior, shutting down or limiting his jaw, lip, and tongue movements.

Difficulties with feeding and oral-motor control are evidenced in the child's inability to coordinate sucking, swallowing, and breathing. Thus, it may take the child an excessive amount of time to drink a minimal amount of liquid.

### Nasal Reflux

Nasal reflux occurs when food or liquid taken into the mouth refluxes upward into the nasal cavity rather than being swallowed. It can be very uncomfortable and can affect the timing and coordination of sucking and swallowing liquids and solids.

Nasal reflux may be an indication of an undiagnosed submucous cleft of the palate. Infants with a cleft of the hard or soft palate do not have the anatomical closure needed to keep food and liquid out of the nasal cavity.

A referral to a physician who specializes in craniofacial disorders may be recommended to rule this out.

### Aspiration

The resistant eater may aspirate or choke due to an absence of or a delayed swallow reflex. Emotional stress often causes physical tension, further inhibiting the ability to protect the airway. Thus, the child who has had a negative experience swallowing food and liquid may tense her body in anticipation of the bottle, cup, or spoon.

The child may also have structural or physiological limitations that influence the ability to protect the airway. Many issues may contribute to an abnormal swallowing pattern, including physical, sensory, and oral control.

If aspiration is suspected, the child should be referred to an otolaryngology, pulmonary or gastroenterology specialist.

**Gagging**

A resistant eater may gag on pureed or lumpy, solid foods. Some swallow the food and then gag, or gagging may occur when the food touches the lips, tongue, palate, pharynx, or esophagus. Gagging may even occur in response to the smell, presentation, or sight of the food.

*FACTORS TO CONSIDER WHEN A CHILD IS GAGGING:*

- Does the child have adequate muscle tone?

  *The timing and efficiency of bolus formation is influenced by low muscle tone, high muscle tone or fluctuating muscle tone. The food can slip into the pharynx before a proper swallow has been triggered.*

- Is the child experiencing sensory defensiveness?

  *A sensory-based gag can occur when the child is hypersensitive in or around his mouth and is unable to manage changes in food texture. The child may also gag because he is unable to tolerate a smell associated with the food.*

- Can the child clear all the food from her mouth?

  *A motor-based gag may occur when the child cannot time and coordinate the bolus formation and swallowing. A partially chewed bolus or parts of the bolus can pass over the back or sides of the tongue before the child is ready to swallow.*

- Is the piece of food too large or inappropriate for the child's developmental age?

  *Some children gag as a way of protecting themselves from food that is too large.*

- Is your child trying to communicate: "I don't want this!"

  *The child may be trying to communicate that he does not like the food or that he feels pressured to eat it. The child may gag due to a gastroesophageal reflux. Understanding the cause of a child's gagging is crucial to preventing a power struggle at mealtimes.*

**Drooling**

The presence of constant drooling during or after a meal or during fine-motor activities after all the child's teeth have erupted is indicative of physical, sensory, or oral-control problems.

A referral to a specialist is recommended if a child drools due to the following causes:

- Nasal congestion and chronic upper-respiratory infections
- Allergy to medication or a side effect of a medication he/she is taking
- Gastroesophageal reflux or aspiration is occurring
- Neurological changes are suspected

Some children lack sensory awareness of the presence of saliva to be swallowed. For example, if a child's face is constantly wet, the sensory cues needed to trigger a swallow may be reduced. Sweet foods trigger more saliva production. Therefore, if a child who lacks sensory awareness eats sweets, he may experience difficulties managing the excess amount of saliva.

Drooling can result from a constantly open mouth, not allowing the saliva to collect and not providing pressure cues to trigger the swallow. An open mouth position may be a result of poor muscle control, poor coordination or low muscle tone.

**Tooth Grinding**

***Victoria***

Some parents feel as if they are going to hit the roof. The sound coming from their daughter is unnerving, to say the least. It never stops and makes other people very uncomfortable when they hear it! Victoria is eight years old and has Down syndrome. Victoria grinds her teeth. When she is told to stop, she starts biting her nails instead. Her parents are spending a fortune on dental care.

Tooth grinding happens when the teeth slide together to make a grinding noise. There are many reasons why children grind their teeth. Some children have poor jaw stability and are unable to grade the opening and closing of their jaw. They often fluctuate between a tightly closed mouth position and grinding their teeth, and resting their jaw in an open mouth position.

Some children who remain on a liquid and pureed diet or whose food selection is limited to soft, mushy foods like yogurt, soft cheese and peanut butter do not regularly receive the proprioceptive experiences other children their age receive from biting and chewing solid or hard foods. When children have missed the developmentally appropriate stimulation received from biting and chewing a variety of foods, they may seek that internal proprioceptive input by grinding their teeth.

The eruption and growth of new teeth provides children opportunities to explore and discover new and different auditory and tactile sensations. Sometimes children grind their teeth because they are exploring, playing and entertaining themselves. Teeth grinding becomes a concern when chronic grinding occurs. It causes the teeth to wear down, reducing the alignment of the child's teeth for biting and chewing, and resulting in pain or tenderness in the muscles that move the jaw. Clicking noises when the jaw opens and closes, and headaches (known as temporomandibular joint syndrome), also occur.

**Limited Upper-Lip Movement**

With limited upper-lip movement the child's lips may not close efficiently during swallowing or when producing sounds. This, in turn, interferes with the development of sucking and swallowing skills, removal of food from a spoon, and efficient biting and chewing.

One of the causes might be a hypersensitivity to tactile stimulation. That is, if the child shows signs of sensory defensiveness, the lip may pull away from tactile contact with the spoon, cup or finger food. Another cause may be that the lips and cheeks are floppy because of low tone. Movement may be limited because of not enough tension in the face. On the other hand, the lips and cheeks may be tight because of increased tightness in the face.

Many children develop an overbite malocclusion of the teeth because of decreased inward pressure from the upper lip. Once this has happened, the child may experience difficulties actively involving the upper lip in feeding and speech movements.

Poor upper-lip mobility and control may compromise the way the child eats and produces sounds and words.

**Immature Spoon Feeding Skills**

***Samantha***

Samantha is a very active two-year-old. Her feeding takes a long time. Samantha uses limited jaw, tongue, lips and cheek movements when taking food from the spoon. When she tries to swallow the food in her mouth, she uses an in-out tongue movement. Samantha's mother always scrapes the food off the spoon using Samantha's upper teeth. Samantha's upper lip does not come forward and down to remove the food from the spoon. Food is usually all over her chin and lower lip, causing her mother to constantly wipe her mouth. Samantha's lower lip does not draw inward to be cleaned by the upper incisors.

The developmental age when the upper lip moves forward and downward to clean the spoon is six to eight months of age. The cleaning of the lower lip only occurs at age 10 to 15 months. Before Samantha will be able to effectively spoon feed, the answers to the following questions regarding her oral-motor skills should be yes:

- Has she developed the ability to use her lips together to support the spoon and remove the food from the bowl of the spoon?
- Is she able to move her upper lip separately from her lower lip?
- Does her top lip move as a whole instead of having stability at the corners of the mouth while the central part of her lip is mobile?
- Has she developed stability in her lower jaw while her mouth is open so that she can separate the movement of her top lip?

By the age of 12 months, typically developing children demonstrate adequate oral-motor skills to remove soft, solid foods from a spoon. Resistant eaters may experience delays in their oral-motor development further compromising their ability to eat the expected quantity of food or doing so with the expected skill level of peers their age.

**Immature Cup-Drinking Skills**

***Dominique***

When Dominique, 15-months-old, is given a cup to drink out of, his initial reaction is to turn his head or clamp his mouth closed. When his parents insist and pour his favorite juice into the only cup he likes to use, he takes a sip by placing his tongue beneath the

***Dominique cont.***

cup while his jaw moves up and down. Not surprisingly, more than half of the contents in the cup end up all over his shirt. Very frequently, Dominique chokes when trying to drink from a cup.

Cup-drinking skills evolve around the age of six to nine months. Children who experience the difficulties described in Dominique's case may not have developed the oral-motor control necessary to drink from a cup. Nevertheless, their actions and preference for bottles or sippy cups may be interpreted as willful noncompliance.

Factors contributing to immature development of cup drinking skills include:

- Sensory – The child cannot tolerate the sensation of the cup on his lips, triggering sensory defensive reactions.
- Physical – Low muscle tone affects the child's ability to control his lips and cheeks.
- Oral control – Lack of jaw stability compromises the development of skilled lip and tongue movement. The child may not have the lateral stability provided by the corners of his lips to support the cup. The timing of the drinking coordination may be too slow to manage thin liquids.
- Preference – Some children lack the ability to generalize the sensorimotor aspects of coordinated drinking from different types of cups.

Many factors can stand in the way of the child's developmental progression to drinking from a cup. Careful observation and assessment should take place before assuming that the child is just being noncompliant.

**Immature Biting and Chewing Skills**

> ***Johnny***
>
> When the spoonful of food is placed in Johnny's mouth, he always bites down on the spoon.

> ***Sherry***
>
> Sherry always bites her cup while she drinks.

A stability bite is often indicative of low muscle tone. Low muscle tone affects a child's posture. The force of gravity on a low-tone body causes the shoulders to fall forward. At the same time, the back is usually rounded, the jaw is pushed forward, and the neck is in hyperextension.

This position often causes the jaw to remain open. Not surprisingly, a lot of effort is necessary to chew or drink in this position. Thus, stability biting may be an effort to gain oral-motor control by recruiting more muscle tone. In this case, the child also experiences difficulties grading her jaw movements especially in the midranges of jaw movement.

If the child is not registering or receiving adequate proprioceptive feedback from the muscles and joints surrounding the jaw, he might use more force in closing his mouth. The child may feel unstable or may need more sensory feedback that tells him what his jaw is doing.

Biting on the edge of a cup for stability is part of the child's normal development. Stability biting becomes a problem when it interferes with the child's ability to take in food in a rhythmical fashion or when the development of internal jaw stability does not occur.

***David***

David is two-years-old and has a diagnosis of autism. He sucks or suckles on any food that enters his mouth. His mother complains about the limited variety of foods he can eat and watches other mothers who are able to give their two-year-olds crackers or apples to eat.

Controlled biting patterns develop between 9 and 12 months of age. By 24 months the child is able to bite most foods using a controlled, sustained bite and starts to grade the jaw opening to the appropriate size for foods of different thicknesses.

A variety of issues may contribute to difficulties biting pieces of food:

- Physical – The child may not have enough teeth to adequately bite into the foods that require advanced cutting or tearing.
- Sensory – Children who avoid lumpy foods and foods that break and scatter on the tongue such as crackers, experience oral sensory defensiveness. These children might avoid biting solid foods because it means that the solid food will turn to a lumpy consistency.
- Oral-motor – The child might experience difficulties inhibiting his tongue movements or stabilizing the jaw in an open position for biting.

If the resistant eater shows signs of sensory or oral-motor dysfunction, he/she should be assessed by an appropriate multidisciplinary evaluation team using the appropriate assessment tools and clinical observations from trained professionals. Careful analysis of the assessment findings will enable the team to determine an effective treatment approach. Chapter Six provides goals and strategies for implementing an individualized treatment plan.

# CHAPTER SIX

## Designing and Implementing a Comprehensive Treatment Plan

Each child who experiences problems with eating is unique and therefore requires an individualized plan to meet his or her needs. A comprehensive treatment plan includes a multilevel and multisensory approach that requires a commitment from parents and the professionals working with the resistant eater. A written plan takes into consideration the strengths and needs of the family and creates a balanced approach that can be easily implemented across settings. For school-age children, it is important that the school team create opportunities to implement the plan during the school day.

Each child is different and the goals for the treatment plan must reflect the unique characteristics of the child. Nevertheless, there are some general goals for all treatment plans.

These include:

1. To create a safe, positive, and nurturing mealtime environment
2. To expand the child's responsibility in preparing, consuming, and cleaning up at mealtimes

3. To improve the child's oral-motor development
4. To address all physical needs of the child during eating
5. To provide multisensory exposure to new foods
6. To respect the child's communication and response to eating
7. To expand the child's repertoire of foods and create a balanced diet

It is important to remember, a written treatment plan is a visual reminder to the team of their commitment and therefore is more likely to increase the success and outcomes for the child. The plan is not intended to be an adverse program that forces or bribes the child to eat. Throughout, the focus is on exploration and learning about new foods and eating. We have found it helpful not to focus directly on the child's mouth but to consider the whole child when developing the plan. The long-term goal is to provide a positive and loving environment for working with the child and supporting his or her eating needs.

Designing and implementing a treatment plan for resistant eaters is not a one-size-fits-all approach. As we have seen in previous chapters, resistant eaters are a heterogeneous group and require a variety of strategies depending on their needs. A comprehensive treatment plan provides the team with the strategies and supports to assist the child at their own pace. The written treatment plan will focus on three primary areas:

**Part 1: Environmental Controls**

**Part 2: Physical and Oral-Motor Development**

**Part 3: Stages of Sensory Development for Eating**

Each area of the plan may be addressed individually or all may be implemented simultaneously. Parents and professionals should prioritize the needs of the child and implement a plan that will be effective for the learning pace of the child.

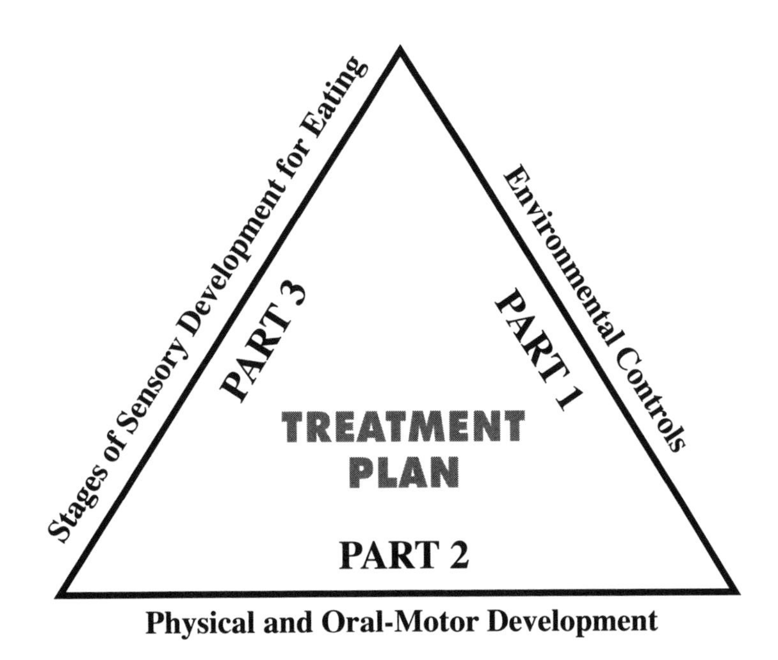


The treatment plan provides the family and professionals with specific goals in each of the primary areas. It is important for all involved to take the time to write out a detailed plan that can easily be implemented. The plan is not intended to include rigid and inflexible deadlines. The focus should be on learning new skills and exploration without the insistence of meeting an arbitrary timeline.

Before we proceed with the treatment plan, we understand that there may be times when neither the school or the family is able to participate in the development and implementation of the treatment plan. Although unfortunate, it should not prevent a treatment plan from being developed. As a matter of fact, school professionals and clinicians have a unique opportunity to implement treatment strategies without the emotional turmoil and stress often related to parenting a resistant eater. Although the goal is for a collaborative multidisciplinary team approach, food aversions and food selectivity can be effectively addressed outside the home with appropriate supports and services. On the other hand, it may be impossible for school personnel to implement a feeding program. Parents should not be deterred from implementing a treatment plan solely in the home.

A sample treatment plan is provided on the following page. The plan includes three general goals and specific activities for meeting each goal. The plan may include fewer goals during the initial phases with additional goals added.

## Treatment Plan

(The following tables will be used as samples and filled in later)

| **Table 6.1** *Part 1: Environmental Controls* |
| --- |
| **Goal 1: To provide the family with a consistent schedule** |
| Activities:<br>• Write down the times for all meals and snacks<br>• Post the schedule in several locations around the house<br>• Use a timer to let everyone know when the next meal will occur |
| **Goal 2: To create an appropriate setting** |
| Activities:<br>• Clean the kitchen table of all unnecessary junk and books<br>• Eat all meals and snacks at the kitchen table |
| **Goal 3: To reduce screaming and crying at the table** |
| Activities:<br>• Avoid coercion<br>• Write out behavior rules and post near the table<br>• Allow the child to participate in setting the table and serving the food |

| **Table 6.2** *Part 2: Oral-motor/Positioning* |
|---|
| **Goal 1: To improve chewing skills** |
| Activities:<br>• Create a "mouth box" filled with chewable toys<br>• Practice chewing foods that are safely wrapped in a BabySafe Feeder/porous bag<br>• At snack time, use foods that increase extended chewing skills |
| **Goal 2: To provide postural support** |
| Activities:<br>• The child's feet are on a stable surface<br>• Make sure the child's hips, shoulders and head are in alignment to support effective and safe eating and swallowing<br>• Table top is the right height for the child to freely use his/her arms during eating |
| **Goal 3: To reduce screaming and crying at the table** |
| Activities:<br>• Wheelbarrow walking<br>• Wall pushups<br>• Carrying grocery bags |

| **Table 6.3** | ***Part 3: Stages of Sensory Development for Eating*** |
|---|---|

**Goal 1: To create a food rich environment**

Activities:

- Purchase plastic foods and play with them during the day
- Read books about food and nutrition
- Sing songs and rhymes that refer to foods and eating (i.e. Apples and Bananas song)

**Goal 2: To increase acceptance of a new food**

Activities:

- Allow the child to shop for a new food
- Place the new food item near or on the child's plate during dinner time
- Allow the child to kiss the food goodbye and throw it in the garbage

**Goal 3: To minimize opportunities for food jags**

Activities:

- Make small changes to the preferred food item
- Include the child when making changes to their preferred food
- Introduce a new brand of the preferred food item

**Guidelines for Writing a Treatment Plan**

1. **The first step in a mealtime treatment plan is to examine the eating habits and beliefs of all of the adults involved.** Whether you are a parent or professional, it is important to review your own eating style. First, take care of your nutritional needs. Second, acknowledge your cultural roadblocks to eating. Third, make a plan to ensure that you are a healthy and balanced role model for the resistant eater.

2. **Create a support network which includes spouses, relatives, teachers, and other individuals who are close to the child.** A child who has experienced many years of problem eating has created defense mechanisms that are difficult to change. A supportive group of family and friends will assist you in your goal of implementing a positive and nurturing feeding program.

3. **Change takes time, so take it slow.** Keep in mind that some of the eating problems your child is experiencing may have persisted for many years, and therefore it will take time to change. Overcoming personal beliefs and cultural roadblocks is a lifetime commitment. It may take a year or longer after a program has been initiated before significant changes in eating will occur. Remember, the child will set the pace for implementation of the plan. Be flexible; not rigid. If something is not working for the child, reassess your plan and identify more practical approaches.

4. **Individualize the plan to meet the needs of both the family and the child.** Although part of every plan requires a written mealtime schedule, the schedule will be different for

each family and child. For example, there may be times that do not allow for everyone to sit down to dinner at the same time, and that's OK. The key is to create a schedule the family can comfortably live with and embrace on a daily basis.

5. **If you skip a day or are inconsistent, get back on plan and pick up again.** Nobody is perfect, and there will be days when the treatment plan is not implemented. Vacations, holidays, and illness will disrupt your ability to be consistent with the plan.

6. **When writing a treatment plan, begin by prioritizing the needs of the child and the family.** As illustrated, each area of the plan includes several goals and activities. In order to avoid feeling overwhelmed, select only two or three goals to implement at a time. In our enthusiasm to "fix the problem," we sometimes attempt to address all the areas at once. It is better to select a few goals at a time before moving on to the next set of goals.

7. **Have fun learning about new foods.** Problem eating is a serious issue and can create a great deal of stress for the entire family. After years of trying to "get the child to eat" a normal diet, parents often feel overwhelmed and at the end of their rope. The first step in the treatment plan is to have fun with food and not focus on eating or putting foods in the mouth. The treatment plan must be child-centered with a focus on age-appropriate sensory activities and playfulness. Exploration and a supportive learning environment are critical.

***Denise***

Denise is the mother of a five-year-old girl with developmental delays. Her daughter is a resistant eater and has a restricted diet of approximately 10 items. Denise would begin fixing supper and feel a knot in her stomach caused by nerves. "I was stressed all the time. As soon as I got home from work, I started worrying about dinner because I knew the tantrums would begin." The negative environment within the home was felt by all the family members. "I know my daughter must have sensed my stress and it just made things worse," Denise acknowledged. Denise reported that after her daughter attended a food clinic and the parents began changing their attitudes and beliefs towards eating, the family mealtime environment was much more relaxed and fun.

Denise and her family are an example of how one family member's problems with eating can affect the whole family. The treatment plan, to be discussed in detail in the following chapters, is intended to provide a new framework for the family to design a supportive eating environment.

***An Exercise in Eating***

Create a written contract for the entire team. The team should include parents, teachers, and other adults who will be interacting with the child on a daily basis. Be sure to also include grandparents. Although they may have the best of intentions, grandparents can inadvertently sabotage a treatment plan by providing unhealthy snacks or catering to the child's rigid food requests. (A sample contract is included in the Appendix.)

## Conclusion

A comprehensive treatment plan is written to support the individual child and family in teaching new eating skills and learning about new foods. Due to the unique nature of resistant eaters, each plan will vary depending on the needs of the child. However, the three parts of any plan will include: environmental controls, physical and oral-motor development, and stages of sensory development for eating. A written treatment plan is a visual reminder to the multidisciplinary team of their commitment to the child.

# CHAPTER SEVEN

## Part 1: Environmental Controls

The first area to address in the treatment plan is **environmental controls**. Environmental controls include scheduling meals, selecting an appropriate setting, creating a supportive climate, designing meals and portion sizes, and addressing food jags. Parents and professionals working with resistant eaters should spend considerable time ensuring that these practical guidelines are being consistently implemented. Environmental controls are the foundation for a solid treatment plan. In order for the child to learn about new foods, the mealtime environment must be positive and nurturing.

***An Exercise in Eating***

A candlelight dinner, a picnic at the park, or maybe a large family gathering during a special holiday—what is your ideal mealtime environment? Describe the perfect meal. Who is in attendance? What are you being served? What is the climate or atmosphere for the meal? Identify those characteristics of this meal that make it perfect for you. Now decide how you can recreate this same scenario at your dinner table at home. What strategies can you implement to create this same atmosphere for the resistant eater?

## Snack and Mealtime Schedules

One of the most challenging aspects of the plan is designing a consistent and balanced mealtime schedule. It is often difficult for families to create a consistent schedule when trying to balance work, school, and extracurricular activities. However, no matter what the lifestyle of the family is, a consistent and predictable daily routine is at the crux of the treatment plan. Resistant eaters need to know when each meal and snack will occur.

## Guidelines for Creating the Meal/Snack Schedule

1. **Write a schedule that is understandable and clear to the child.** If the child has limited reading skills, a picture schedule should be utilized. Post the schedule where it will be visible to the child and other family members.

2. **Use a timer to indicate when the next meal/snack will begin.** Some children struggle with the concept of time and do not understand what it means when the parent states, "dinner is soon." A kitchen timer can help make the concept of time more concrete.

3. **Use a kitchen timer during the meal to set the pace and the length of the meal.** Depending on the child's age and developmental level, a meal should last between 15-30 minutes. If the child is still eating an appropriate and balanced meal after the timer goes off, the parents should use common sense and be flexible and allow the child to finish his meal. If the child is in school, he or she will need to follow the school's schedule for eating in the cafeteria.

4. **Make sure the mealtime schedule includes snacks**. Snacks are given the same priority as a meal. Snacks should consist of balanced and healthy choices. Snacks are usually offered twice per day. Be flexible, some children may require more scheduled snacks per day based on their age.

5. **Make the meal/snack schedule different for each child depending on medical status, age, and weight.** Most children under the age of five follow a meal-snack-meal-snack-meal schedule. This type of schedule allows for ample opportunities to learn about new foods and ensures adequate food intake. If the child has medical problems or a lower percentile for weight, the schedule may include more opportunities for exploring and eating foods throughout the day, yet without continuous grazing. Specific gaps in time are included in the schedule when the child is not eating. School-age children do not always receive snacks during the school day and, therefore, may need an additional snack after the last meal.

6. **Offer the child at least one preferred food item at every meal and/or snack.** This is critical to the success of the plan. The treatment program is not intended to starve the child or limit food intake. Therefore, it is necessary to include foods the child is willing to eat at every meal along with new foods for the child to explore (See Food Selection).

7. **Provide only water to the child between the scheduled meal/snack time.** This guideline is not intended to be harsh or punitive. Instead, the goal is to set clear limits

for eating and to limit grazing. The overall effectiveness of the treatment plan is compromised if the child is allowed to graze between meals and eat during unscheduled periods. If the child is consistently hungry at a certain point in the day, change the schedule so she receives a meal/snack at that time. The goal is not to stress the child or cause anxiety but to provide a helpful and supportive schedule.

***Shawna***

Shawna's mother picks her up from school at 2:30 P.M. and takes her directly to swim lessons. Her mother knows that Shawna will be hungry when she picks her up, so she brings her an apple (not a preferred item) and corn chips (one of her preferred foods). Shawna's mealtime schedule reflects that her snack will be at 2:45 P.M., on the way to swim lessons and dinner will be at 5:00 P.M. Shawna regularly refuses to eat the apple and will only eat the corn chips, so invariably she is hungry when she gets home from swimming at 4:00 P.M. Shawna walks in the house from swimming stating, "I'm hungry." Her mother is consistent and follows the schedule. She reminds Shawna in a neutral voice, "Dinner is scheduled for 5:00 P.M. You can have a drink of water and wait until dinner." Her mother also sets the timer so Shawna has a visual support to let her know when dinner will begin.

Shawna's mother is not being punitive nor is she trying to win a power struggle with her daughter. Children who are resistant eaters need limits and a consistent schedule for eating. Typical snack foods generally consist of sweets or carbohydrates and do not provide a balanced and healthy meal. If Shawna's mother attempted to give her an additional snack after swimming, Shawna would less likely be hungry one hour later for dinner. Shawna's mother may reconsider changing the schedule on swim days and move dinner to 4:30 P.M. if Shawna is consistently hungry. The goal of the mealtime schedule is for the child to have an understanding of when food will be offered and to minimize any confusion or anxiety. The parents are responsible for creating an appropriate schedule and consistently following the schedule on a daily basis.

### The Mealtime Setting

A mealtime setting may include eating in the car on the way to school, at a baseball game, or at the dinner table. For most families, the setting varies according to their schedule. For resistant eaters, the setting must be predictable and consistent. The setting determines the tone of the meal. A comfortable and supportive setting will help the child relax and focus on learning new skills to eat. A consistent mealtime setting should be approached similar to the schedule. During the first stages of the treatment plan, the child may not be willing to be present or be comfortable at the dinner table due to past negative experiences. The dinner table may be associated with pressure and punishment so it will take some time for the child to trust the setting and begin to explore new foods.

### Guidelines for Selecting a Setting

1. **Eating and drinking is to be done at the table.** The optimal mealtime setting is the dinner table. As will be discussed later in Chapter Eight, the dinner table provides the child with the appropriate supports and helps to maintain an appropriate posture position. Also, it provides much-needed structure for the resistant eater. Children should

not be allowed to walk around the room while eating or drinking their meal/snack. At first the child may associate the dinner table with past negative experiences. It may take a few weeks before the child can relax and sit at the table without anxiety.

***Crystal***

Crystal is a petite four-year-old with a limited diet. Her parents often have meals at the dinner table but Crystal refuses to sit down. Instead, she roams around the kitchen occasionally stopping to pick food off of her plate. The parents explained that Crystal will eat at the table when she goes to her grandmother's house. After further examination, the parents realized Crystal was roaming around the room at home because she was expected to sit on the full-size kitchen chair without any physical supports or a booster seat. On the other hand, grandma allows Crystal to use her high chair, which gives her support and appropriate positioning. A simple change in seating arrangements made a big difference for Crystal and her family.

2. **The amount of distractions at mealtimes should be kept to a minimum.** While some children can eat a balanced diet in front of the television, resistant eaters need to focus on the process of eating. Allowing resistant eaters to watch television during meals will only support their continued rigidity and food aversions. The meal should occur in an environment that focuses on eating and socialization. Whether at the dinner table or in the school cafeteria, the setting should be relaxing and supportive for the child.

3. **Parents, siblings, and peers play an important role during the meal.** The setting should include other family members or peers. If the child is eating alone, she is missing opportunities to socialize. Emphasize the importance of family time.

The goal when selecting a mealtime setting is to ensure it is relaxing and physically supportive so the child can learn new skills and explore new foods. The setting may change for every meal. Breakfast may be at the kitchen counter, lunch in the school cafeteria, and dinner at the dining room table. However, whatever the setting, be sure the child has the physical supports to explore and learn about new foods successfully.

### Create a Supportive and Nurturing Environment

A supportive and safe eating environment is one in which the child feels respected, nurtured, and trusted to explore new foods and learn new eating skills without coercion, deception, and/or punishment. The goal is to create a climate of caring and support and respecting the child's ability to feed himself. It is only when parents and professionals are able to allow the child to accept responsibility for what he eats and how much he eats, that the child can begin to explore new foods. A supportive environment is without punishment and coercion and allows the child to take the lead in learning about new foods.

### Guidelines for Creating a Supportive Mealtime Environment

1. **Respect the child and do not invade his mouth without permission.** Respecting the child's responsibilities for eating and learning about foods is the cornerstone of

an effective treatment program. Food is not to be placed in the child's mouth without permission. Some children are not able to give their permission verbally, but may have to show they are ready by leaning towards the food and opening their mouth. In the beginning of the treatment plan children may be testing the adult to be sure they are not going to be coerced or forced to eat. Parents and professionals must repeatedly assure resistant eaters that they will not be forced to eat anything before they are ready.

2. **Role-play and demonstrate eating techniques.** Resistant eaters can be influenced by strong role models during meals. Role models are important during mealtimes. Give the child an opportunity to role-play being the parent. For example, she can serve the food and even dish out the portion sizes to each member of the family. The child may also be given the opportunity to feed others at the dinner table. This type of role reversal can be very empowering for the child who has experienced little power around the dinner table.

3. **Never discuss the child's eating habits or how much she eats during the meal.** The conversation at the meal should be positive. Snacks and mealtimes are an opportunity to share the events of the day. This is not a time to focus on the resistant eater.

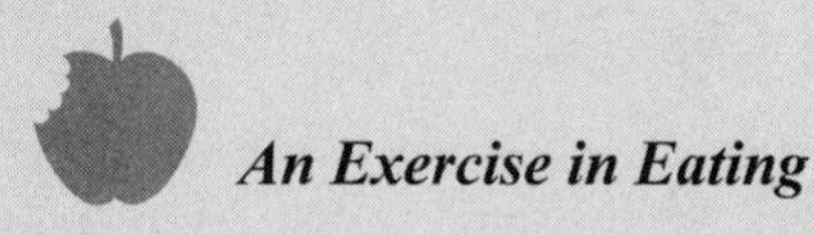

*An Exercise in Eating*

Create colorful visual reminders of what mealtimes should be all about. These posters can assist all the family members in focusing on positive outcomes around the dinner table. For example, "Food is Fun" posters should be visibly displayed as a reminder to parents who may subconsciously fall back on old patterns of coercive behavior. Design a large poster with Ellen Satter's (1987), *Division of Responsibility*, motto. All of these visual reminders will assist the adults and encourage the resistant eater.

4. **Discuss the taste, texture and smell of new foods.** Parents, peers, and professionals should explicitly describe what they are eating and the process of eating. For example, "I am using my front teeth to bite off a piece of this apple. Then I have to use my tongue to place the apple on my back teeth." Or, "Chewing a piece of cracker is very easy because it dissolves in my mouth. But I have to chew longer with a piece of hamburger before I can swallow it." It is important for the child not to eat alone on a consistent basis. Whether in a school setting or at home, the child should eat with others who can role model the different aspects of eating.

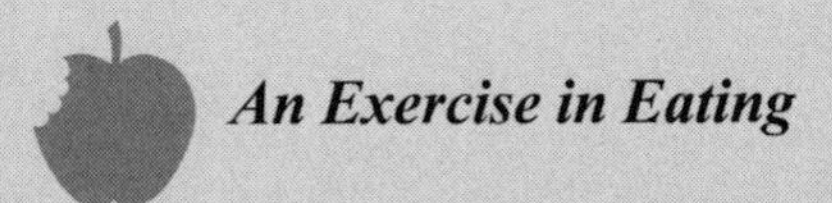

***An Exercise in Eating***

Videotape a mealtime with the child to use as a future teaching tool. Children love to watch themselves on video. Discuss what you are eating and the taste and textures of the foods. Pay special attention to the different smells of the food. Role play being the parent and child and allow the child to take the lead. The child can then watch the video over and over again while learning about new foods.

**Portion Size and Food Selection**

The words "biggie size" and "jumbo" are ever-increasing in our food vocabulary. Portions of foods served at restaurants have doubled in size in the last five decades. Thus it is not uncommon these days for restaurants to serve one meal on a large platter that could serve a whole family. Our society has lost track of what an appropriate serving size is, and we often pass those miscalculations on to our children. If a normal-size dinner plate is filled with food and placed in front of a child who is a resistant eater, he will be overwhelmed with the amount and unsuccessful in his ability to eat. The portion size should be presented in a manner that allows the child to be successful. Children must be served age-appropriate portions of food.

**Guidelines for Implementing Appropriate Portion Sizes**

1. **Provide the child with an age-appropriate size plate and utensils.** Dinner plates have gotten larger over the years. For a three, four, and five-year-old, the size of a normal dinner plate is too large and overwhelming. Begin by selecting a smaller size lunch

plate or salad plate. Consider purchasing small plates that display a favorite cartoon character or animal. The smaller plates with child friendly pictures will assist the child when eating.

2. **It is better to start the meal with a smaller portion size as it allows the child to see the results when taking a few small bites.** The goal is for the child to feel successful eating a new food. If the child loves pizza but will not eat carrots, give her a full slice of pizza and a small portion of carrots. A teaspoon of carrots is sufficient when first learning about new foods. By keeping the portion size small, the child will more likely feel capable of trying the carrots.

3. **A good rule of thumb for controlling portion size is to consider one tablespoon of each type of food for each year of the child's age.** For example, a four-year-old would receive approximately four tablespoons of a fruit or vegetable during a meal or snack.

As mentioned, several studies have shown that portion sizes have increased dramatically over the past 50 years. An adult-size portion of food will be considerably greater than a child's size portion. Yet, we often serve adults and children the same amount of food. The following table provides guidelines for serving sizes for children. Keep in mind that these are only suggestions and that all children are different. The goal is to offer child-size portions. Children who experience problems with eating may begin with an even smaller portion size as they are learning about new foods.

| **Table 7.1** *Serving Sizes for Children* | | | | |
|---|---|---|---|---|
| | **Age 1-3** | **Age 3-5** | **Age 6-8** | **Age 8+** |
| Meat, poultry, fish | 1-2 Tbsp | 1 oz | 1-2 oz | 2 oz |
| Eggs | 1/4 | 1/2 | 3/4 | 1 egg |
| Cooked dried beans | 1-2 Tbsp | 3-5 Tbsp | 5-8 Tbsp | 1/2 c |
| Pasta, rice, potatoes | 1-2 Tbsp | 3-5 Tbsp | 5-8 Tbsp | 1/2 c |
| Bread | 1/4 slice | 1/2 slice | 1 slice | 1 slice |
| Vegetables | 1-2 Tbsp | 3-5 Tbsp | 5-8 Tbsp | 1/2 c |
| Fruit | 1-2 Tbsp | 3-5 Tbsp | 5-8 Tbsp | 1/2 c |
| Milk | 1/4-1/3 c | 1/3-1/2 c | 1/2-2/3 c | 1 c |

***An Exercise in Eating***

Do you know the actual amount of one ounce of meat or 3-5 Tbsp. of fruit? Our society has supported larger sizes in recent years and forgotten the importance of appropriate portion sizes. Place measuring cups, measuring spoons, and a small scale on the table. Work with the child to serve an appropriate portion size. Make a game of it. At first guess how much a 2 oz. serving of meat would be, then measure it to see if you are correct. Introduce opportunities of making it fun to guess the correct serving size.

**Food Selection**

Food selection is another area of concern for families with resistant eaters. After a resistant eater repeatedly refuses to eat new foods, parents often begin to fix only the foods the child prefers. As discussed in the next section, parents should not cater to a child's rigid food requests. On the other hand, it is important to select foods that may be characterized as child-friendly. Consider the child's age and eating abilities when buying and preparing food for the family. Keep in mind that new and exotic foods can be a scary adventure for the child.

**Guidelines for Food Selection**

1. **Select only one menu for the entire family.** A family meal should include a protein or meat, starch, fruit, and/or vegetable, and milk. The menu should include a variety of foods familiar to the resistant eater as well as some new foods. Do not buy and prepare separate meals for the resistant eater. Remember the division of responsibility by Ellen Satter (1987), "Parents are responsible for what foods are purchased and prepared for the family. The job for the parent is done when the food is placed on the table."

2. **Select foods that are child-friendly.** Child-friendly foods do not have to be overly processed or unhealthy. Grilled chicken, small boiled potatoes and peas are examples of child-friendly foods. Purchase and prepare foods that taste good to the entire family. The family menu should include foods that are not only nutritious but satisfying and taste good.

3. **Consider texture, color, and smell when introducing a new food.** Exotic foods with strong odors may not be the best place to start when introducing new foods. Also, some foods are easier to chew and swallow than others. At first, a thick steak or corn on the

cob may be too difficult for a resistant eater to chew and swallow. Food selection should be carefully considered.

4. **Include a piece of bread or roll with meals.** Children are often successful at eating breads and rolls. Thus, a meal that includes bread allows the child to be successful.

5. **Be flexible!** Although an effective treatment program should be implemented consistently, there will be times during the week when it is impossible to prepare a healthy and balanced meal. There will also be mealtimes when the family does not all eat the same foods such as when going out to a restaurant. It is important to remember the goal of the treatment plan is for long-term and permanent changes in eating habits. Occasionally missing one balanced meal or occasionally providing only preferred items to the child will not cause a total failure of the program.

6. **Remember that food selections in school may be limited to the items served in the cafeteria.** Children who experience problems with eating may be hesitant to eat the cafeteria food. School personnel should work with the parents in selecting a lunch menu that will provide opportunities for learning about new foods. Teachers can also speak to the cafeteria staff about selecting some food items for exploration in the classroom.

Food selection is an important part of the treatment plan. Catering to a child's food rigidity will continue to support inflexible food choices. Select new foods that are child-friendly and will increase opportunities for learning to eat new foods. While the treatment program is being implemented and the child is learning about new foods, the menu should always include at least one preferred item. Children should be offered at least one food at every meal that they can readily eat and enjoy. The long-term goal is to increase the variety of foods and to fade food aversions. The focus of each meal should be a balanced and healthy diet.

***An Exercise in Eating***

Children should be included in the menu planning process. Although parents are ultimately responsible for the menu, children can be included in selecting new and favorite foods. Have each member of the family select his or her favorite meals. Be sure to provide them with the guidelines for selecting a healthy menu (meat, starch, vegetable and milk). Have each member of the family review the grocery store advertisements and coupon section from the newspaper. Even very young children can be involved with looking at the variety of foods and selecting foods for the weekly menu.

**Food Jags**

A food jag refers to the insistence on the same food, or the same serving utensils, or even the same setting over long periods of time. Many parents report that resistant eaters not only require the same foods prepared in the same manner but also require the same plate and spoon at each meal. A classroom teacher recently reported that a child in her class required the same seat for lunch and demanded the same plate and cup sent from home. The teacher noticed that any slight changes to the routine caused the child to have a tantrum and refuse to eat. Every day the teacher made sure no other child sat in the special seat in order to prevent any problem behaviors.

Like this well-intentioned teacher, parents can exacerbate a food jag by supporting the child's rigidity in order to minimize problematic behavior. When food jags are supported by the adult, the resistant eater becomes more rigid in his eating patterns. It is important to vary the foods presented to the child, even if the variations are only slight changes.

**Guidelines for Addressing Food Jags**

1. **Create opportunities for structured flexibility and choice making.** Structured flexibility allows the child to have some choices while maintaining the structure of the schedule and selecting from a list of healthy choices. Provide the child with choices for plates, utensils, and cups. Be sure to acknowledge and support the child's ability to handle change.

2. **Do not cater to the child's rigidity in wanting only the same foods.** Make slight changes in the presentation of the food. If the child is demanding macaroni and cheese every day for dinner, start by selecting different brands of macaroni and cheese, or use different kinds of noodles. Another way of changing the macaroni and cheese is to add a small amount of food coloring. This does not change the taste but adds variety. Be sure the changes are small and do not create anxiety for the child.

3. **Include the child in food preparation and presentation.** The child should also be involved in making changes to the preferred food items.

Food jags are a normal developmental stage for two- and three-year-old children who fear new foods. It is important to acknowledge the child's food preferences while introducing new foods. However, parents and professionals should resist the temptation of supporting the child's rigidity and instead offer some flexibility into the child's eating program.

### Appropriate Behavior During the Mealtime

Although a child-centered and nurturing approach is the foundation for a comprehensive treatment plan, the mealtime environment must not be disrupted or impaired by a resistant eater or any other member of the family. This same rule applies to students in the cafeteria. The goal is to create a calm and supportive atmosphere without disruptions or inappropriate behaviors. Parents and professionals must set consistent and age-appropriate rules and boundaries for the entire group. For example, a three-year-old cannot be expected to remain at the dinner table for 30 minutes while mom and dad have finished eating and are talking. Set the timer for 15 minutes and after the child has completed her meal, let her clean up her plate and leave the table. Again, using common sense will assist families in creating appropriate behavioral expectations for the meal.

### Guidelines for Implementing Appropriate Mealtime Behaviors

1. **Resistant eaters often exhibit challenging behaviors during mealtimes due to their persistent food aversions.** For any challenging behaviors that have been occurring

for months or even years, it will take some time to extinguish and replace them with appropriate behaviors. Be patient. If the mealtime environment is supportive and the child is not forced to eat, the child will quickly learn new and appropriate behaviors for eating.

2. **Set up a routine for transitioning to the table.** Create a checklist for the child to help prepare for the upcoming meal. The before meal routine may consist of: (a) wash hands, (b) select plates and utensils for the meal, (c) put food items on the table, and (d) pour a drink. Mealtimes will be smoother if the adult provides a plan for the transition period.

3. **If the child exhibits noncompliance or tantrums during the meal, calmly remove him or her to a safe area away from the group.** The adult working with the child should remain calm and without judgment. Let the child know that his behavior is sending a message that lets you know he is not hungry or that he is finished. The rest of the family or group continues with their meal without the child.

4. **If a child leaves the table prior to completing the meal or if the child has had to be removed from the table due to problem behaviors, do not allow him to return to the meal.** This may seem harsh at first, but with consistent implementation of this rule the child will learn that he must remain at the table in order to eat. This is not a punitive action. Remain neutral and let the child know he will not be eating until the next scheduled meal or snack.

5. **If the child throws food or destroys food, he must clean it up.** The rule of natural consequences suggests that a child must repair any damage or mess they have created.

6. **Analyze your judgment about the child's behavior.** Are you filtering your expectations of the child through your cultural beliefs? Parents and professionals need to accept some appropriate playing with food or making a mess on clothes. If a child is consistently being removed from the table, the rules and parents' expectations may need to be adjusted to meet the child's needs.

***An Exercise in Eating***

Develop consistent and age-appropriate rules for the mealtime environment. The rules should support the child's need for learning about new foods. All adults working with the resistant eater should consistently implement the rules at every snack and meal. A few examples of rules for a meal are:

1. Keep food on your plate.
2. Use a utensil to serve food from a bowl.
3. Remain in your seat until the timer rings.
4. Let an adult know when you are done. Use your words or a picture card for "Finished."
5. Place all unused food items in the trash can.

The written and/or visual rules should be posted and in clear view of the child at every meal.

All family members present at the meal should follow the established rules. The rules and boundaries written for mealtimes should be child-friendly and support the resistant eater. It may take several days before the child understands the rules and their natural consequences. Remain calm and provide adult consistency during this learning period. If problematic behavior continues after 7-10 days, review the mealtime climate and setting. Consider the following questions related to troubleshooting persistent problem behaviors:

1. Does the child receive at least one preferred food item at every meal?
2. Is the positioning and seating appropriate for the child's size?
3. Is the environment stress-free and relaxed without any coercion or pressure to eat new foods?
4. Is the child empowered to end the meal in a positive manner such as handing the adult a card that says "Finished" or asking to leave the table?

Significant lifelong change takes time. Some resistant eaters have never successfully sat at the table for an entire meal. Celebrate the small successes along the way.

## Conclusion

Environmental controls include the schedule, setting, portion size, and food jags. Parent and professionals must pay special attention to creating a mealtime environment that is consistent and nurtures the child's strengths and weaknesses. It is also important for the plan to include behavioral expectations for both the family and the resistant eater. Parents and professionals should soon witness changes in the child's approach to mealtimes and learning about new foods. If the parents and professionals have ceased all attempts at coercion and bribery, the resistant eater should begin experiencing success with new foods.

If at any time during implementation of the plan, the child becomes stressed or anxious, or if you feel you are working against the child, slow down and reevaluate. The child is probably communicating that his or her needs are not being met. Watch carefully for the signs and take the child's lead. The timeline for implementation of the feeding plan is based on the child's needs, and some resistant eaters may be experiencing severe delays in oral-motor development or have not been given appropriate physical supports at mealtimes. Part 2 of the treatment plan will address these issues and provide a variety of activities for the home and school.

# CHAPTER EIGHT

## Part 2: Gastrointestinal, Physical and Oral-Motor Development

Chapter Seven addressed how to set the foundation for a solid treatment plan, namely addressing the environmental controls which include scheduling meals, selecting an appropriate setting, creating a supportive climate, designing meals and portion size, and addressing food jags. Environmental controls set the stage for creating a positive mealtime environment.

It is important to remember that the timeline for implementation of the feeding plan is based on the child's needs and developmental readiness. As discussed in Chapter Five, many resistive eaters may be experiencing mild to severe gastrointestinal discomfort. They may experience minimal to severe delays in oral-motor development or they may not have adequate postural control or have been given appropriate physical supports to promote their successful participation in mealtimes. This chapter will therefore address part two of the treatment plan, namely:

1. Gastrointestinal comfort
2. Adequate postural control and positioning
3. Oral-motor function

A variety of activities for home and school are included to address postural control and oral-motor development.

**Gastrointestinal Comfort**

Treatment of gastroesophageal reflux (GER) can be as conservative as positioning the child in a vertical/upright position during and after meals or as invasive as surgery. Children with GER benefit from reduced meal sizes and they should avoid spicy, fatty and acidic foods such as citrus fruits. Medications are often used to manage GER. The most common are: over-the-counter antacids such as Mylanta and Maalox which neutralize stomach acid; acid inhibitors such as Zantac suppress acid production in the stomach; acid blockers such as Prevacid or Prilosec completely block acid production in the stomach; motility drugs such as Reglan increase the muscle tone of the digestive tract, and anti-ulcer drugs such as Carafate. Surgery is usually considered in life-threatening situations such as chronic aspiration or vomiting and when the condition cannot be managed with positioning or medications. A procedure called a fundoplication is performed in which a portion of the very top (fundus area) of the stomach is wrapped around the lower esophagus to tighten the malfunctioning sphincter valve. This allows food and liquid to enter the stomach from the esophagus, but tightens the sphincter so that food, liquid and air cannot move upward to reflux.

It is important to reduce the stress around mealtimes. Carefully observe the child for any signs of GI discomfort, such as grimacing, increase in body tension, wiggling, shifts in attention, rumbling sounds in the stomach, coughing and changes in the swallowing of saliva. When these initial signs of discomfort appear, initiate strategies to improve comfort such as reminding the child to breathe more deeply, putting gentle pressure on the abdomen, gentle movement, or listening to music that is calming. Another important strategy to promoting gastrointestinal comfort in the older child is to teach them to distinguish a stomach that hurts from a stomach that is hungry. Further information on resources can be found in the Appendix, at the end of this book, and in Chapters Twenty-Two and Twenty-Three in *Pre-Feeding Skills: A Comprehensive Resource for Mealtime Development, 2nd ed.* (2000) written by Suzanne Evans Morris and Marsha Dunn Klein.

***Logan***

Four-year-old Logan, sits in a high chair at the table with his brothers for a meal. His feet don't touch the floor and he has to constantly be reminded to stop kicking the table with his feet. The high chair provides some support for Logan's body. However, he continues to slouch and his mother has to adjust him frequently because otherwise he starts sliding under the tray. He is given a teaspoon and ravioli in one bowl and applesauce in another bowl. He taps the ravioli with his spoon, but doesn't seem to know how to scoop the large pieces of pasta on to his spoon. He attempts the applesauce instead. He holds the spoon in a fisted grasp and brings the spoon up to his mouth. Most of the applesauce lands on his shirt and chin because he doesn't lift his elbow high enough or bend his wrist enough to turn the spoon to get into his mouth. Further, the little bit of applesauce that actually landed in his mouth stays there until he takes a sip of water to wash it down.

The position of the child's body can affect his or her eating skills. As in the case of Logan, when a child's body does not have sufficient stability, it expends more energy, working harder to find ways to stabilize the body—having to lift the arms higher than necessary and knowing where the legs and feet are. Also the child's attention and focus is on his body and perhaps the discomfort he is feeling, rather than on the food and the mealtime experience.

During Logan's occupational therapy, he was showing great gains in eating larger amounts of food at mealtimes. It was quite a puzzle to the therapist to learn that this was not the case at home until she made a home visit and realized the differences in Logan's seating arrangements between the clinic and home. At the clinic, instead of being wedged in between the tray and the backrest of his high chair, Logan sat on a bench, giving his body a chance to move, which helped Logan stay alert and attentive to the meal, and his feet were on the floor. Logan did not kick his feet against the table because he was receiving enough proprioceptive input through his feet and legs to know where they were in relation to the rest of his body. Also, he never slipped under the table because he was receiving the stability he needed by having his feet firmly on the floor. Further, Logan's body was able to remain upright and he could lift his elbow higher. Finally, less food was spilled and more food was getting into his mouth. The therapist observed that in a stable position like the one in the clinic, Logan was more capable of using increased jaw movements and was attempting to chew foods he always refused at home.

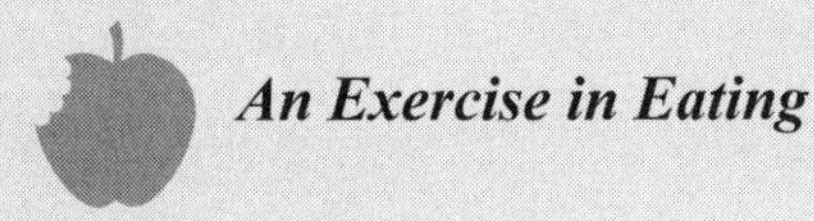

### *An Exercise in Eating*

Try to sit on a tall chair where your feet cannot touch the floor. Take note of your body position and which parts of your body you move or hold tight in an effort to compensate for your dangling feet. Now bend your back into a slouched position and take a drink from your glass. It's really hard to tilt your head backwards when you are in this position, isn't it?

Our body has learned to automatically adjust itself so that we alleviate any feelings of pain or discomfort, and automatically learns to realign itself for safe and effective swallowing of food and liquids.

When a child's body does not have adequate control and stability, or when the child is not aware of the position of the parts of her body, she will find it difficult to control the movements used to feed herself. Furthermore, if she is placed in a high chair or strapped to a bolster seat in which she cannot move to adjust her body or in which her feet are not on a stable surface, she might find it hard to eat or drink because she is experiencing discomfort or her body is not aligned properly for easy eating and swallowing. No matter the child's age, when working with resistant eaters it is important to take a look at what the child is seated in, how his body is positioned and whether he is receiving enough stability to free his arms to bring food up to his mouth and allow his head to be upright for his oral-motor skills to function adequately.

As a child grows and gains more motor control over his body, he will not necessarily need such a stable position for eating. For example, walking into a teenager's room one day, a mother was surprised to see her daughter lying on the bed, her head hanging upside down off the side of her bed, while she was talking on the telephone and eating a piece of pizza at the same time. When the child has muscle tone issues or postural control problems, that compromises his ability to align his head and body so that he can chew, drink and swallow effectively. He uses all his efforts and focuses on his body instead of enjoying the mealtime experience.

This chapter will first examine how the position of parts of our bodies (body alignment) can influence our eating skills, followed by a series of lessons and activities designed to strengthen muscles and consequently improve posture. From looking at larger muscle and motor development, we go on to discuss oral-motor development, again supported by a series of activities designed to help the child function better, especially when it comes to eating.

## Physical Development

### The Upper Body

The shoulders play an important part in eating because they enable the child to get his hands to his mouth, put his hands together and reach for a toy. Think of the shoulders as the base or floor upon which the head and neck sit. If there is not adequate balance, with the shoulders providing a stable base for the head and neck, the muscles moving the lips, cheeks, jaw and tongue will move inefficiently. To further complicate matters, the child's lips need to develop graded fine-motor movements apart from the tongue or the jaw or cheeks as part of the process of eating.

If the shoulders are rounded forward in a slouched position, the head will automatically be pulled forward and tilted downward. Taking a sip of water in this position will force the head to have to work hard at tilting backwards, the throat will feel a tight pull as the chin is raised. In this position, the lips, tongue and jaw cannot work effectively to manage the liquid.

***An Exercise in Eating***

Take a sip of water but before you swallow, tilt your head backwards and stick your chin up in the air. Now try to swallow. Difficult, don't you think? Take note of your own position when you take a sip the comfortable way. You are usually sitting upright and you tuck your chin in slightly. Keep this position in mind when you watch your child drink.

To have good head control, you have to have an active, flexible spine. The neck has to do all the work of controlling the head if the spine is rigid or fails to work as a coordinated unit. Further, if the muscles in the neck are not strong, they fatigue easily, especially when they have to take full responsibility for maintaining the head in an upright position.

***An Exercise in Eating***

Have you ever been on an amusement park ride where your trunk and shoulders are tightly strapped in? What does your head and neck feel like after the ride?

When a child is positioned or strapped into a tightly fitting chair so that spinal movement is difficult or even impossible, the full spine cannot assist in controlling the head.

Moving down the body, our trunk, the part of the body between shoulders and hips, must be stable in order for our arms to work efficiently. The trunk supports us so that we have an upright posture. For example, when you reach for the salt, the trunk bends just enough for you to reach the salt by extending your arm. The trunk does not move all the way with your arm, otherwise you would fall over! Trunk stability is important in order to be able to use our arms effectively. Some children with decreased trunk stability may benefit from added support such as a towel roll wedged on the sides of the body or behind the back.

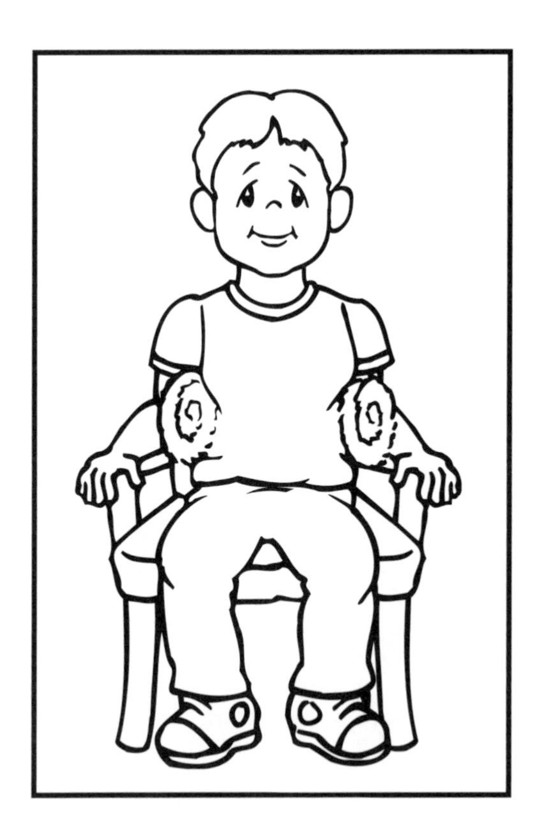

When it is necessary to provide added seating support to promote trunk control during eating, at school or for transportation, it is important to remember to include activities to develop mobility and control through the entire spine.

***An Exercise in Eating***

Sit upright and reach with your arms above you and out to the sides. Now slouch over and try to move your arms in the same way. Finally, lean to one side with your trunk and move both arms. You will probably find that you cannot reach as far when you are in a slouched position.

**The Lower Body**

While it may not seem obvious, the position of the pelvis has an effect on head control, breathing, voicing, and mouth control. That is, as the pelvis is tilted in any direction, the spine makes changes to accommodate the trunk. The child may find it more difficult to breath when he is compensating for the imposed spinal curve or position. In the same way, the child's shoulders, head and mouth are affected during sitting.

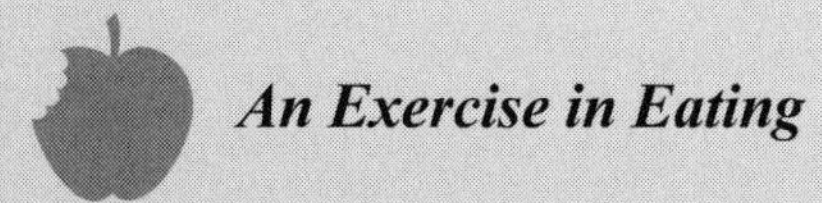

***An Exercise in Eating***

Take note of how you breathe when you are sitting up straight. Now change your position and bend your shoulders forward, shifting your hips and pelvis so that you have a rounded back. Breathing may become more shallow or it may take more effort to take deep breaths.

The child's feet can support his legs and help provide the stability and balance his body needs for good oral-motor skills. Dangling feet in a chair that is too high can prevent the child from obtaining stability in his hips, pelvis, trunk and head. Lowering the chair so that the feet touch the floor or providing footrests can make a huge difference in promoting balance and stability during mealtimes, as we saw with Logan earlier in this chapter. When the child has sufficient stability in his body, he is able to use his body more efficiently and will not have to focus or work so hard at using other body parts to help him stay in an upright position for eating.

## Postural Control Activities

The following lessons and activities are designed to improve the child's posture by strengthening muscles that work at providing postural control. When the child is demonstrating significant problems related to how she moves her body or is unable to stabilize her trunk, a referral should be made to an occupational or physical therapist who can assess the child's motor skills and provide a more specific exercise program.

**Goals for Postural Control:**

1. To improve awareness of posture and strengthen the muscles which assist in postural control
2. To strengthen the shoulders, trunk, pelvis and legs
3. To improve shoulder stability and strength
4. To improve postural control, muscle tone and general endurance

## Lesson 1: Postural Control

Materials:

- Child-size chairs

Procedures:

1. Child sits on a chair with his/her feet resting on the floor.

2. Ask the child to bring one leg up to the chest and squeeze/hug the leg, and then drop the leg to the floor.

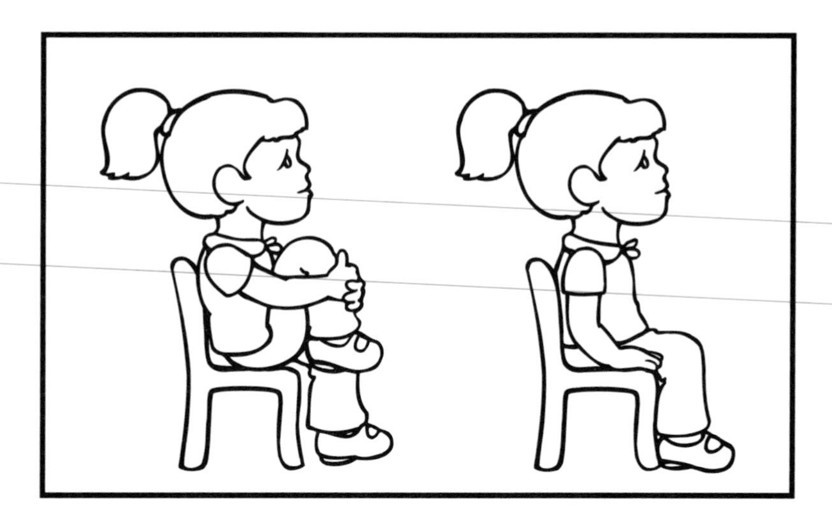

3. Ask the child to bring the other leg up to the chest and squeeze/hug the leg, and then drop the leg to the floor.

4. Have the child bring both legs up to the chest, hug/squeeze both legs, and drop both legs to the floor.

5. Ask the child to touch her shoulders to her ears by squeezing the shoulder and neck muscles tightly, drop her shoulders and make them soft and relaxed.

6. Ask the child to put the palms of her hands together, push her hands tightly together and then make them soft and relaxed.

**Lesson 2: Upper Body and Shoulders**

Materials:

- Picture cards found in Appendix

Procedures:

1. Wheelbarrow walking – ask the child to get into the crawl position, pick up the child's legs, supporting at the knees. Ask the child to "walk" on their hands. If the child keeps the elbows in a straight, locked position, ask him/her to bend the elbows slightly. Wheelbarrow walking is often used as an event in school field days. Relay races while

wheelbarrow walking can be played. An obstacle course in which the child has to weave in and out of cones is another idea.

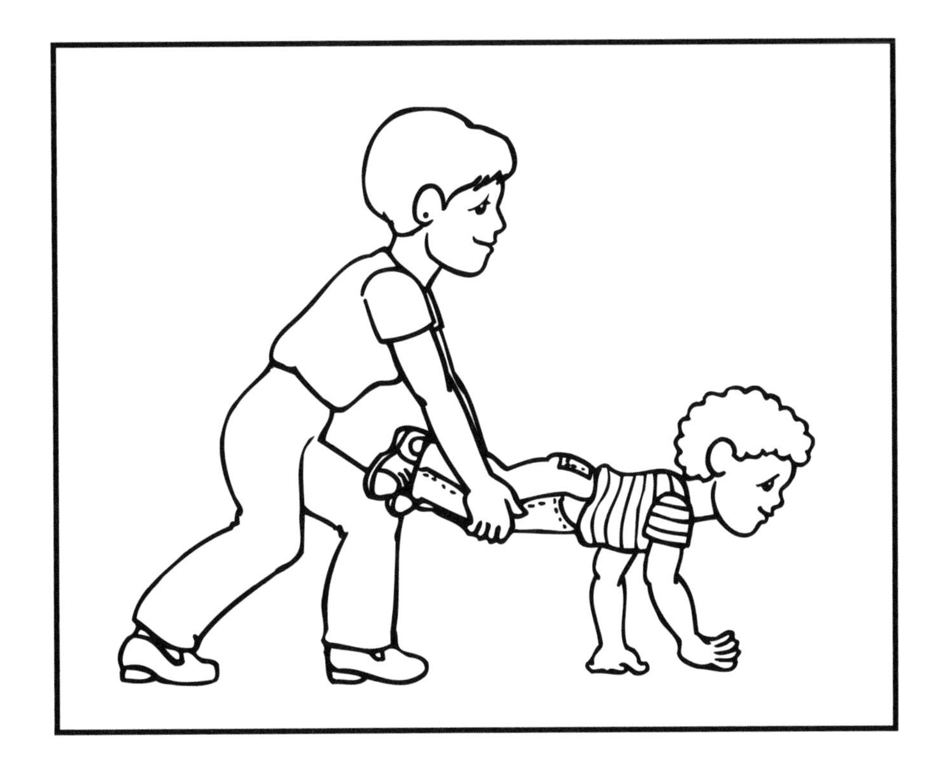

2. Donkey kick – the child assumes the wheelbarrow walking position and kicks his/her legs up in the air. The child can play with kicking one leg and then the other and then both legs at the same time.

3. Tug-o-War – take a towel and knot the ends. One child holds one end and another child holds the other end. They pull to see who can pull the other one to their side. (This is a great activity for sensory defensive children as it provides proprioceptive input without direct touch.)

**Lesson 3: Coordination and Motor Planning**

Materials:

- Scooterboard
- Cones
- Jump rope

Procedures:

1. Ask the child to lie on his stomach on the scooterboard and, using his arms, propel the scooterboard around the room.

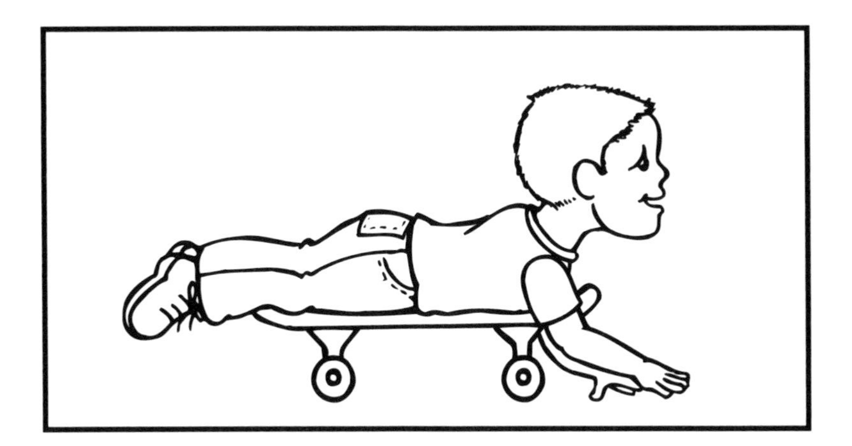

2. Place cones around the room for the child to weave in/out of, and around like an obstacle course.
3. Child/adult holds a jump rope at one end, and the child on the scooterboard holds the other end. The person standing pulls the child around.

4. Have the child maneuver the scooterboard on different surfaces to provide varied resistance. For example, the child will use more effort in propelling the scooterboard over a carpeted area than over a smooth linoleum surface.

## Lesson 4: Upper Body Strength

Materials:

- Picture cards - see Appendix
- Pillows

Procedures:

1. Crab walk – assume position as illustrated in picture.

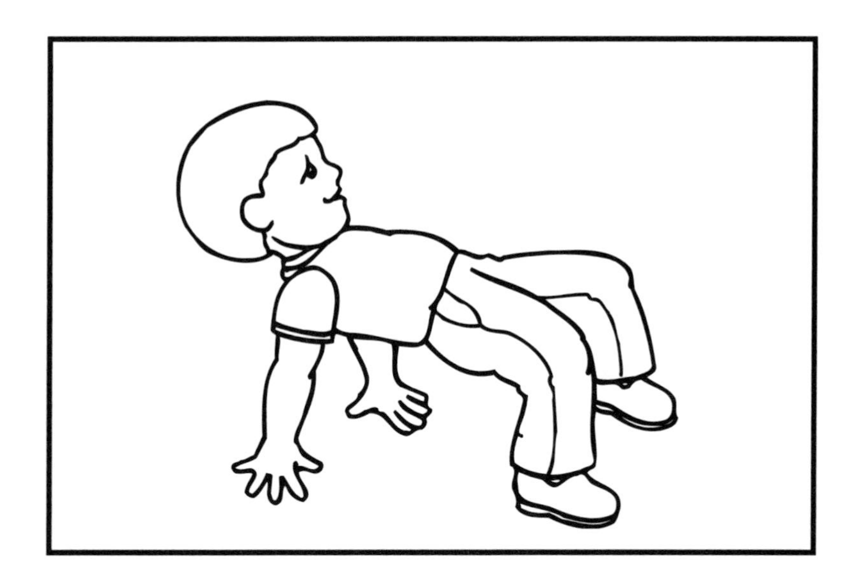

2. Bear walk – assume position as illustrated in the picture. Remember to keep the legs straight.

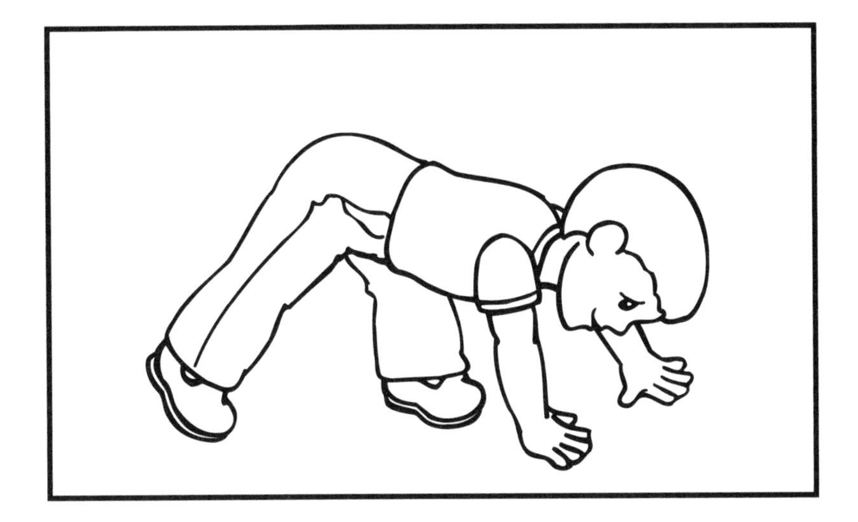

3. Inchworm walk – ask the child to assume the bear walk position, walk hands out as far as possible, then walk the feet forward as close to the hands as possible. Repeat the inchworm action.

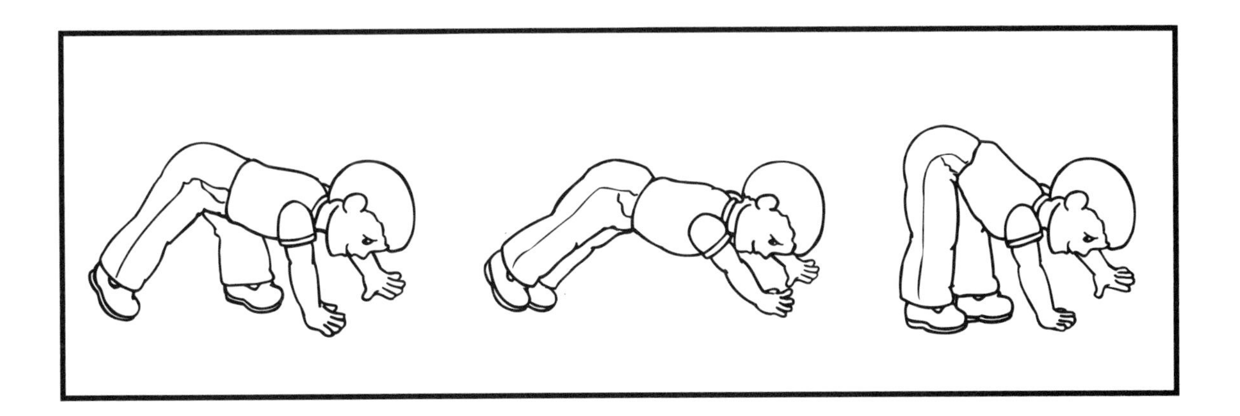

4. Have a pillow fight.

5. Wall pushup – ask the child to stand facing a wall. Explain that you want his/her help to make the room bigger, so the wall has to be pushed back. Ask the child to place his/her hands against the wall and push as hard as he/she can.

**Lesson 5: Heavy Work Activities Around the House**

Materials:

- Common household chore items:

  Broom, dust cloth, watering can, furniture, grocery bags, etc.

Procedures:

1. Ask the child to perform household chores, for example:
   - Help wash the car
   - Dust furniture
   - Push the chairs in after meals

- Wipe off the table after meals
- Sweep the floor
- Carry the watering can and water house/garden plants
- Carry grocery bags from the car to the kitchen
- Pour the water/juice during snack time

## Oral-Motor Activities

The emphasis on incorporating oral-motor activities into the child's routine is not to make the caregiver's life more complicated than it is already. These activities have been carefully chosen so they can easily be implemented into the child's daily routine. For example, while the child brushes her teeth, she can work on building awareness of her mouth and explore moving her tongue from one side to the other, during the drive to school, she can sing silly songs with facial actions. Specific oral-motor exercises to address issues such as those discussed in Chapter Four (namely abnormal sucking pattern, nasal reflux, aspiration, gagging, drooling and tooth grinding), should be referred to an occupational therapist or speech and language pathologist who is specifically trained in oral-motor intervention techniques.

Many different methods are utilized in the treatment of oral-motor issues and it is suggested that parents work closely with the professionals to carefully choose which one is most beneficial for their child. Some interventions use facial massage or stretching of the muscle fibers of the cheeks and lips, others incorporate the use of equipment such as whistles, straws, and so on, to improve oral-motor skills.

Remember, it is up to the child to give permission for the adult to enter his/her mouth. The parent/teacher/therapist must be sensitive to the child's cues and wait for the child to give permission by leaning slightly forward and opening his/her mouth. If your child does not allow the therapist to put her fingers in her mouth, for a given intervention, it may be a sign that it is not the right approach at that time. When choosing an oral-motor program for a child, the parent, teacher, or therapist should ask the following questions to make sure the program is appropriate:

- Is the child giving me permission to do this technique in and around his/her mouth?
- What structure(s) am I facilitating? (lips, tongue, jaw, etc.)
- What process(es) am I facilitating? (breath control, eating, drinking, etc.)
- What am I working on (improving awareness, muscle tone, strength, stability, mobility, control)?

**Goals for Oral-Motor Programs:**

1. Increase sensory awareness of how the body moves and that it can move "separately" or as a whole
2. Normalize muscle tone in the jaw, lips, tongue and cheeks
3. Increase active movement of the tongue, lips and cheeks
5. Improve spoon-feeding skills to develop a mature pattern of removing soft foods from the spoon that includes upper-lip movement to remove food from the spoon and drawing in of the lower lip for cleaning by the upper incisors

6. Improve cup-drinking skills to develop an organized rhythmical pattern of sucking and swallowing when drinking liquids from a cup
7. Improve straw-drinking skills
8. Improve biting and chewing skills

**Lesson 1: Awareness and Dissociation of Movement**

Materials:

- Child size chairs
- Emotions pictures - see Appendix for pictures to copy and laminate

Procedures:

1. Ask the child to scrunch eyes, nose, cheeks, and mouth together to make them tight, then make them soft by relaxing the muscles.
2. Ask the child to scrunch eyebrows, forehead and eyes tightly together, and then make them soft.
3. Ask the child to make her eyebrows rise up and her eyes open wide, and then make them soft.
4. Ask the child to smile.
5. Imitate a sad, happy, angry, surprised face. Explain the different parts of the face and how to do different actions.

**Happy:**

Cheeks tightly squeezed

Eyes relaxed/soft

**Sad:**

Corners of the mouth turn down

Eyelids close half way

Eyebrows pull together

**Angry:**

Lips squeeze together tightly or

you show teeth with your lips apart

Eyes tighten

Eyebrows pull together

**Surprised:**

Mouth is wide open

Eyes are wide open

Eyebrows are pulled upwards

### Lesson 2: Normalize Muscle Tone in the Jaw, Lips and Cheeks

Materials:

- Washcloth
- Facial vibrators such as crocodile/elephant
- Face paints or washable bath crayons

Procedures:

*Younger Children:*

1. Play patty-cake, peek-a-boo, row-row-row your boat and similar children's games to incorporate patting, tapping, and stroking, as well as tactile and proprioceptive stimulation of the muscles that open and close the jaw.
2. Ask children to sing while you touch and tap their face. Use music with a clear rhythm and regular tempo during tapping.
3. Play peek-a-boo using a washcloth on the child's face. Pull the washcloth off the child's face using both your hands and simultaneously touching the face and gently drawing the cheeks and lips forward to form the lip rounding position to say "Boo."

*Older Children:*

1. Explore while the child is washing his/her face. Ask the child what it feels like when rubbing slowly, then rubbing fast; rubbing softly, then with firmer pressure; while tapping on the face.
2. Adult does "animal walks" on the child's face. For example, an elephant walks with slow heavy feet, a mouse walks fast and lightly.
3. Using the vibrating crocodile/elephant, "walk" around and explore the "mountain" (nose), or the "caves" (nose).
4. Using face paints or bath crayons, draw on the child's face, and have him rub it off without looking in a mirror.
5. Draw shapes on the child's face, and have her identify them.

## Lesson 3: Muscle Tone in the Tongue

Materials:

- Washcloth
- Toys with textured surfaces
- Spicy/bitter foods (atomic fire balls, hot tamales, hot gum balls, red hots, cinnamon powder)
- Sour/tart foods (lemonade powder, Tang powder, tear jerkers, sour gummy worms, raisins, shock tarts, sour patch kids, war heads)

Procedures:

1. Ask the child to identify the specific area of the tongue you have touched or to indicate whether there was one touch or two.
2. Explore different textured toys, smooth surfaces, bumpy surfaces etc. If the child is comfortable, he/she can play this game with eyes closed and be the detective.
3. Explore different spicy, tart, bitter or sour foods by placing the food on different places on the tongue and in the mouth.
4. Use vibration with a small massager (i.e. an electric toothbrush on the tongue or under the chin).

### Lesson 4: Movement for the Tongue, Lips and Cheeks

Materials:

- Mirror
- Variety of sauces or salad dressings

Procedures:

1. Child dips his/her finger in a sauce or salad dressing, and licks it off each finger.
2. Child explores his/her fingers by feeling them with his/her lips.
3. Child counts his/her teeth with his/her tongue.
4. Child makes different shapes with his/her lips for example: fish lips.
5. Have child make sounds with lips: smacking, humming.
6. Have child make clicking noises with the tongue like the gallop of a horse.
7. Tell the child to pretend there are strings attached to her cheeks, forehead and chin. Have the child pull the forehead string up or down (move her eyebrow up/down). The child can pull each string individually or together.

Remember to cut the child's fingernails when you include activities that encourage moving the hand to the mouth. Scratches and jabs are uncomfortable and can discourage future play and exploration.

**Lesson 5: Spoon-Feeding Activities**

Materials:

- Different spoons with different bowl depths to stimulate more lip activity during spoon feeding:
  - Deeper bowls require more upper-lip activity during spoon feeding.
  - Shallow bowls require less upper-lip activity during spoon feeding.
- Different foods to provide varying degrees of resistance during food removal:
  - Liquids require little effort as they can be poured into the mouth.
  - Yogurt and pudding are smooth and provide limited resistance.
  - Honey, jam and peanut butter provide strong resistance, and challenge the upper lip to work harder.

Procedures:

1. Pause with the spoon at the child's lips or on the tongue so that the child has time to close his lips around the spoon for food removal. When the spoon is removed too quickly, the child tends to rely on the adult to scrape the food on the upper lip or teeth.
2. Present the spoon laterally instead of directly placing it straight into the child's mouth and on the tongue. Rest it gently on the lower lip, with the spoon bowl resting on the lip corners. The contact with the lip corners provides extra stability for the upper central lip to be more active in food removal. Pause with the spoon in this position, enabling

the child to use his upper lip to actively come down to remove the food. This sideways presentation enables the child to use his lips to remove the food and begin the suck-swallow process. It also helps keep the tongue inside the mouth. A flat-bowled spoon works well for this activity.

### Lesson 6: Cup-Drinking Activities

Materials:

- Strained fruits or vegetables mixed with a small amount of liquid—use with a child who is familiar with the foods and likes them
- Milkshakes, blended smoothies, applesauce diluted with other liquids, and blenderized fruits and vegetables
- Cutout cups and cups with a wide or flared shape—enable the child and adult assisting to see the liquid as it approaches the child's mouth. Some cups have lids that control the liquid flow, while still allowing the child to feel the lip of the cup.

Procedures:

1. Use a thickened liquid to facilitate learning cup-drinking skills. The child receives more sensory information from the thicker liquid, and it does not run into and around the child's mouth as quickly as thin liquids do.

## Lesson 7: Straw-Drinking Activities

Straw selection for children with oral-motor challenges depends on whether the child can control his/her lip movements and at the same time coordinate his/her breath.

Materials:

- Straw
- Cup
- Liquid

Procedures:

When the child is starting to learn to sip through a straw:

1. Put a straw in a glass of liquid. Put your finger over the top end of the straw, keeping the liquid in the straw. With the straw slightly greater than horizontal, put the straw to the child's lips. As the child closes his mouth around the straw, take your finger off the straw end and let the liquid move into the mouth. Gradually move the straw to just below horizontal to enable the child to suck the liquid through the straw.

2. Gently squeeze a juice box, a soft plastic bottle, or a sports bottle to bring the liquid up a straw with a one-way valve such as the "Sip-Tip Cup" straw system to the child's mouth.

After the child has mastered drinking with a straw, the following variations and activities can be implemented to improve the child's oral-motor skills:

1. Have the child suck different thicknesses of liquids, purees, puddings, slushes or applesauce mixed with apple juice from a straw.
2. Have the child drink from short straws, long straws, wide and narrow straws. Use colored straws, straight straws and curly straws.
3. Have the child suck from different positions on the lips: the center, side and in between.

4. Play "vacuum cleaner" – Have the child suck a piece of paper up to a straw and "carry it" to a different place and then let it go.

**Lesson 8: Biting and Chewing Activities**

Children with oral-motor difficulties often resist foods that require extended chewing. Chewing is a partnership between the tongue, the jaw and the cheeks. Follow-through with some activities listed in Lessons 2, 3 and 4.

<u>Materials</u>:

- "Chewy Tube"
- Polyester organza material cut into squares or "Baby SafeFeeder"
- "Mouth Box" (see Appendix for suggestions for contents)
- Raw carrots, raw celery, beef jerky, licorice twists and sugar-free bubblegum

Procedures:

1. Place a soft toy or a "Chewy Tube" between the child's teeth or gums in the molar region. Encourage the child to make biting or chewing motions on the toy. Please note that the child practicing any biting and chewing activities with soft toys needs constant supervision to ensure that the toy does not break into small pieces and get swallowed accidently. Change the used toys that are starting to wear.
2. When the child is practicing a chewing motion with food, wrap a bite-size piece of food in a thin, porous bag (made of polyester organza or cheesecloth) or use the Baby SafeFeeder. Place the food bag between the teeth to simulate chewing. In this way, the child can taste the flavor of the food and practice chewing on it without the risk of pieces of the food breaking off.

3. Create a "Mouth Box" filled with chewable toys to be used whenever appropriate. Keep a plastic container so the items do not get left all over the house and become dirty.
4. Ask the child to move long strips of food slowly into the mouth, approaching from the side of the mouth as the child uses a rhythmical biting and chewing pattern. Strips of food that work well for this activity are pretzel sticks, TERRA vegetable stix or cheese puffs.

5. Try giving the child the following kinds of foods at snack time to increase extended chewing and chewing without drooling skills: raw carrots, raw celery, beef jerky, licorice twists, and sugar-free bubblegum.

## Conclusion

In summary, the old nursery song, "The hip bone's connected to the …" demonstrates how every part of our body affects how we position ourselves and adds to our comfort or discomfort. The connectedness of our muscles affects our oral-motor skills and, ultimately, influences our ability to eat. If the resistant eater is experiencing postural problems, it is important to address them through a comprehensive treatment plan. Likewise, if the resistant eater's oral-motor skills are compromising his ability to manage food in his mouth safely and effectively, he is likely to be more resistant to exploring and accepting new and challenging foods into his diet.

The activities provided in this chapter give parents and professionals a starting point to address and improve postural and oral-motor issues. As mentioned, it is important for the child with more severe postural and/or oral-motor dysfunction to be referred to a trained, experienced professional who will provide a thorough assessment of the child's strengths and limitations and design a specific treatment plan and home program.

# CHAPTER NINE

## Part 3: Stages of Sensory Development for Eating

The final part of the comprehensive treatment plan focuses on the stages of sensory development for eating. Children developmentally learn to accept new foods through their senses. Toddlers often play and experience foods while sitting in their high chair. As toddlers begin to touch and smell new foods they eventually begin to place small amounts in their mouths. Each experience teaches the child about the sight, smell, and texture for each new food. The developmental stages of learning about a new food can be applied to resistant eaters.

***Jessica***

It's Jessica first birthday and all the family has gathered around to watch her blow out the candle on her birthday cake. Mom has made a special cake with whipped frosting just for Jessica to eat by herself. Jessica is loaded up in the high chair and covered with an oversized bib to protect her new pink dress. The party-goers sing the final chorus of "Happy Birthday" and the small cake is placed on the tray of Jessica's high chair. Her brown eyes grow wide as she looks at the cake with hesitation. Slowly but surely she begins to explore the frosting with her fingers. The crowd cheers her on to dig in with

***Jessica cont.***

both hands. She starts to smear the icing on her tray and then in her hair. Flash bulbs go off from the cameras of excited grandparents. Next Jessica gets a big glob of cake in her ear after her hand was clapping with the crowd. Jessica is unsure about having the cake on her fingers, so she attempts to lick off the icing. The chocolate cake and white icing cover nearly every inch of her head and face as she relaxes and explores the cake with both hands.

As a one-year-old, Jessica has demonstrated how she learns to eat a new food. First, she experienced the food by looking at it and tolerating its presence on her high chair. Next she smeared part of the icing on her head and ear so she can begin to understand about the smell and texture of the cake. Lastly, she placed her hands in her mouth to assist her in experiencing the taste and textures.

Children learn to eat new foods through the developmental sensory stages as described in Jessica's story: acceptance, touch, smell, taste, and eating. Children and adults of all ages can learn to acquire new tastes for foods with the appropriate treatment plan. Acquiring a taste for a new food may take several months. Researchers have reported that it may take up to 10-15 exposures of a new food before a resistant eater is ready to move on to the next sensory stage. Therefore, a comprehensive treatment plan should include multiple opportunities for exposure at each level.

**Guidelines for Implementing the Stages for Sensory Development**

1. **Activities and lesson plans for learning about new foods can be implemented either at the end of the meal or at a separate scheduled time dedicated to "Learning about New Foods."** Identify on the schedule a 10-15 minute planned opportunity for implementing the activities.

2. **Select a playful, nurturing, and non-threatening setting.** If you are a therapist or school personnel, the location will be your classroom or clinic. At home, you might consider using a small table away from the dinner table.

3. **Have fun and avoid coercion.** The goal of each lesson is for the child to lead the activities and enjoy learning about new foods. According to Hendy and Raudenbush (2000), a teacher's enthusiasm can greatly increase the chances of a resistant eater exploring and accepting a new food. Strong and enthusiastic role models reduce the degree of neophobia and assist the child in learning about new foods. As mentioned earlier, the use of a puppet as a role model is fun and beneficial particularly for young children.

4. **Use typical peers or siblings for support.** In the home setting, invite one or two typical peers over to participate in the activities. For school settings typical peers may also be invited to play food games and be role models. Be sure to select children who will be supportive and compliant during the session. When typical peers are added to

the group, allow the resistant eater to select the activity for the session in order to be successful.

5. **Select age-appropriate activities.** The lesson plans provided in this chapter cover a wide range of age groups and cognitive abilities. Not all lessons are appropriate for every age group. Parents and professionals can modify lessons to meet the individual needs of the child. Be sure to select the activities which are most appropriate and enjoyable for the child.

6. **It is perfectly alright to repeat the same lesson several times.** Children learn through repetition and enjoy playing games they are familiar with. It may take up to 10-15 times of repeating the same activity before the child is ready to move on to the next sensory stage.

7. **Not all children like the same foods.** We all have our food preferences and likes and dislikes. In order to be considered a "good eater," you don't have to like every food. A good eater is one who enjoys eating, likes a variety of foods from each food group, and can tolerate new foods. If a child truly does not like a food after 10 attempts at exposure, select another food from the same food group.

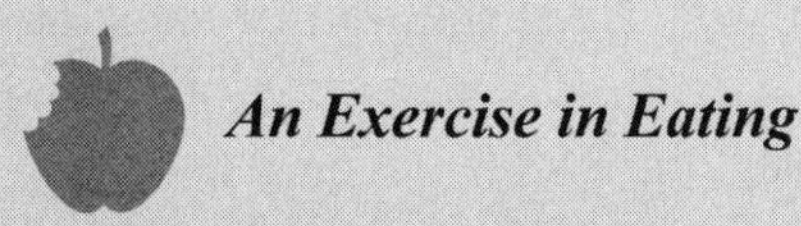

*An Exercise in Eating*

Try role reversal. Allow the child to feed the adult. Be prepared to have fun. Implement this activity during an exploration time and away from the family mealtime. The message to the child is that we are in this together. This activity has the added advantage that it allows the adult to experience what it must be like for the child to be fed, sometimes against one's will, by an otherwise well-intentioned person.

8. **Provide many opportunities throughout the day to learn about new foods.** Learning about new foods does not have to occur only at a mealtime. Be creative and provide a **food rich environment**. This means that a child is exposed to plastic foods in the bathtub/shower, singing about foods in the car, and reading about foods at bedtime. A food rich environment is one where the child feels safe to learn about new foods across settings.

Due to the nature of problem eating and the individualized strengths and weaknesses of each child, it is important to start the journey into learning about new foods in a fun and exciting manner. The following lessons are intended to be playful and child centered.

## Stage One: Acceptance

Stage One of Sensory Development focuses on *acceptance* of new foods. *Acceptance* refers to the resistant eater's acceptance and endurance of a new food in his or her presence while decreasing anxiety during exposure. *Acceptance* can vary from the ability to be in the same room with a new food—to allowing a new food on a serving plate.

### Goals for Acceptance

- To increase the child's willingness to be exposed to a new food
- To increase the child's ability to tolerate being in the same room as a new food
- To increase the child's ability to allow a new food on the table
- To increase the child's acceptance of a new food on the child's plate
- To reduce the child's anxiety of new foods
- To increase the child's awareness of the food groups and the food pyramid
- To increase the child's knowledge of the mouth and the digestive system

The individual child may already accept and tolerate a variety of foods on the table. Some resistant eaters need to spend very little time at the *acceptance* stage, if they demonstrate appropriate skills in this stage of sensory development for most foods. Do not skip this important stage of sensory development, however. Even if the child is more advanced, it is still important to play with new foods and set the framework for future learning opportunities.

### Guidelines for Implementing Stage One-Acceptance

1. **Keep it fun without any coercion to eat a new food.** An adult may have to frequently reassure the child that she will not be forced to eat a new food.

2. **Select activities that are age-appropriate.** As mentioned earlier, not all lessons provided here are appropriate for every age group. Initially, select the lessons which allow the child success so as to build confidence for the future.

3. **Maintain a positive and supportive attitude.** Resistant eaters have had a lifetime of disappointments and anxiety around new foods. It may take several weeks before the child is willing to tolerate a new food.

## Stage One-Acceptance

### Lesson 1: Food Diary

Materials:

- Construction paper
- Lined paper
- Instant camera or digital camera
- Colored markers or crayons

Procedures:

1. The food diary is a visual reminder to the child of all the experiences he will have throughout the treatment program.
2. Construct a small booklet with 30-40 pages of paper. Bind the book using staples or put it in a 3-ring binder.
3. Have the child create a cover by drawing pictures or cutting out favorite foods from magazines.

4. Take numerous pictures of the child at each sensory stage. Have the child glue or tape the picture in the book, and have an adult or the child write a few sentences about their experiences.
5. Read the diary to the child on a daily basis both at home and at school as a reminder of their new learning about foods.

### Lesson 2: The Food Pyramid

Materials:

- Provide a variety of books on the food pyramid
- Copies of the food pyramid (see Appendix)
- Crayons/markers/colored pencils
- Plastic foods

Procedures:

1. Provide the child with a copy of the food pyramid.
2. Using crayons or markers, have the child color each of the food groups.
3. After coloring each food group, have the child select a plastic food and identify the food group to which it belongs.
4. Discuss the special features of each food group such as color and texture.
5. Display the food pyramid in the classroom or kitchen.

### Lesson 3: Hot Potato

Materials:

- Three new foods that are new to the child

- Three foods the child prefers
- One small bowl
- Music

Procedures:

1. Select a variety of fun and age-appropriate music.
2. Sit on the floor, preferably in a small group of 3-4 people.
3. Place one food item in the small bowl.
4. Turn on the music and begin to pass the bowl around the circle, just like the game hot potato. Have someone turn off the music.
5. The person holding the small bowl when the music stops makes a statement about the food item; for example, "the carrot is orange" or "the lemon is round."
6. The person left holding the small bowl selects the next food item and place it in the bowl.
7. The game is finished after everyone has had an opportunity to select a food item.

**Lesson 4: Meet Your Teeth**

Materials:

- Toothbrush and toothpaste for each child
- Set of plastic teeth
- Copy of the mouth
- Crayons/markers

Procedures:

Contact a local dentist for donations of toothbrushes and toothpaste. Also, inquire if the dentist can donate an old x-ray to show children.

1. Provide each child with a toothbrush and toothpaste.
2. Have the children practice brushing the plastic teeth.
3. Have the children color the picture of the mouth and discuss the different types of teeth and their purpose during chewing.
4. Explore the child's mouth with the toothbrush and let the child identify the different teeth and their role in chewing.
5. Display the pictures of the mouth and teeth for the group to see.

**Lesson 5: Cookbooks and Recipes**

Materials:

- Library (if necessary)
- Cookbooks

Procedures:

1. Go to the library and check out several cookbooks if an adequate supply is otherwise not available.
2. Look at the pictures in the cookbooks and identify the food groups with the child.
3. Allow the child to select a few recipes to read.
4. Choose a recipe to make together.
5. Allow the child to participate as much as he is comfortable.
6. Make it clear to the child that he does not have to eat any of the food prepared.

Note: In the classroom, cookbooks are a great source for reading and math activities. Use cooking as a topic for a thematic unit and teach a variety of lessons across subject areas.

## Lesson 6: Grocery Shopping

Materials:

- Grocery list
- Trip to the store

Procedures:

1. Sit down with the child and write a short grocery list (fewer than five items). Try to select foods from a variety of food groups.
2. Take the child to the grocery store.
3. Allow the child as much independence as possible by pushing the cart, finding food on the list, picking up the new items, and paying for the items.
4. Discuss the different food groups in the store.

## Lesson 7: Grow a Garden

Materials:

- Seeds
- Small pots or plastic containers
- Potting soil

Procedures:

1. Show the child the seed packets and allow him to select a few types of vegetables to grow. Try to select a vegetable that will grow easily in your area.

2. Have the child place a small amount of potting soil in the container.
3. Place seeds in potting soil and water lightly.
4. With the child's assistance, keep track of the plant's progress. After a few weeks the vegetable should be ready for picking. A resistant eater may be more willing to taste a new vegetable that he has grown himself.

### Lesson 8: In-School Field Trip

Materials:

- School cafeteria
- Written list of rules and schedule for the field trip
- Small group of children

Procedures:

Be sure to thoroughly prepare the child for a visit to the cafeteria. Provide a visual schedule for the visitation along with a set of written rules that have been verbally reviewed several times prior to the trip.

1. Meet with the cafeteria staff prior to the field trip. Point out that the focus of the field trip is to acquaint the children with new foods and discuss how the cafeteria provides a balanced meal. Ask the staff to have a few foods displayed for the children to see.
2. Visit the cafeteria with the children. View the different foods that are prepared. Review the school menu and discuss the various foods.
3. Have the cafeteria staff tell the children their roles and responsibilities in the cafeteria.
4. After returning to the classroom, review the monthly school menu. Identify the food

groups on the menu.

5. Write a thank-you note to the cafeteria staff.

## Stage Two: Touch

Touching foods is the next sensory stage of development for acquiring a taste for new foods. This stage should not be introduced until the child has reduced his anxiety to new foods and has demonstrated the acceptance skills for new foods. If the child has shown signs of accepting new foods in his environment, it is time to move to Stage Two.

Touching new foods is a very big step for some resistant eaters. Touching can include using the hands, feet, head, or any part of the body. Babies often learn about new foods by smearing it on their high chairs or in their hair. Touching new foods can be approached in a variety of fun and exciting ways.

**Goals for Touching**

- To increase the number of foods the child is willing to touch
- To decrease the child's anxiety when touching a new food
- To explore a new food with hands, feet, and other parts of the body
- To increase awareness of the various textures of new foods
- To provide an environment that encourages exploration of a new food

The sensory stage of touching new foods can be fun but it can also be very messy. Some children find it difficult at first to play with raw cucumbers or lunch meat for example. It is important to remember that the hands have hundreds of sensors and may not be the most appropriate to begin with a touching program.

**Guidelines for Implementing Stage Two-Touch**

1. **If you are implementing this stage in a school setting, have parents send aprons or old t-shirts to protect the child's clothing from being stained.**

2. **Classroom teachers may consider asking the local grocer for free food samples**. At this developmental stage, you may consider using day-old fruits or vegetables to play with and explore because the food will not be eaten.

3. **Ask the school cafeteria for small portions of leftovers to play with in the classroom.**

4. **Be sure to purchase plenty of paper towels and hand wipes for quick clean-up.**

5. **Do not force any child to touch a food if they are uncomfortable.** The child may be allowed to use a pretzel stick or a carrot stick to touch another food during this transition.

## Stage Two-Touch

### Lesson 1: Mystery Item

Materials:

- Covered box with a small hole
- 7-10 food items
- Paper towels

Procedures:

1. Place one food item in the "Mystery Box."
2. Have the child place her hand through the hole and touch the item.
3. Let the child guess what is in the box.
4. Give the child a turn to select and place a food in the box. Now the adult has to guess what it is.
5. Repeat each item several times.

### Lesson 2: Hot Potato

Materials:

- 4 new foods
- 4 preferred foods
- Music
- Small group of children or family

Procedures:

1. Play this game similar to the game in Stage One, but this time have each person hold the food and pass it around the circle.

2. Turn on the music and begin to pass the food item around the circle, just like the game hot potato. Have someone turn off the music.
3. The person holding the food item when the music stops makes a statement about the food item: for example "the carrot is orange" or "the lemon is round."
4. The person left holding the food item selects the next food item.
5. The game is finished after everyone has had an opportunity to select a food item.

**Lesson 3: Painting with Food**

Materials:

- 2-3 different sauces, salad dressings or condiments to be used for "painting"
- 3-5 new foods
- Construction paper
- Paper towels

Procedures:

1. Select 2-3 different sauces that will be used for painting. Condiments such as ketchup and mustard work well, as does ranch dressing, yogurt, or applesauce. As a reminder, if the child "loves" ketchup, use plenty of ketchup for this activity.
2. Select several food items to serve as paint brushes. Food items such as carrot sticks, celery, chicken drumsticks, pretzel sticks and broccoli spears work well.
3. Provide each child with a small bowl of "paints" and food items to paint with. Also provide construction paper.
4. Ask the children to have fun and make beautiful art work.

### Lesson 4: Show and Tell

Materials:

- Have each child bring in 2 foods: 1 new food and 1 preferred food

Procedures:

1. Allow each child to select one food item and stand or sit in front of the group with it.
2. Have the child state one fact about the selected food item.
3. Have each child take turns describing the food item.
4. The child may hide the food item while the group asks questions about the item.

### Lesson 5: Rainbow of Foods

Materials:

- 1-2 foods from each color of the rainbow
- Construction paper
- Glue

Procedures:

Assign each child in the group a certain color food to bring to share with the group. Dried fruits, nuts, and beans work best with this project.

1. Have each child select a piece of construction paper. Tell the children that they will be creating a food rainbow by using different colored food items.
2. Have the child use a small amount of glue to paste the food item onto the construction paper in the shape of a rainbow.

3. Continue to glue each item until the rainbow is complete.
4. Discuss the different textures of each color of food.

### Lesson 6: Science Experiment

Materials:

- 3-5 foods with seeds or kernels (apples, cucumbers, watermelon, avocado, oranges)
- Plastic knives or scoops
- Paper towels

Procedures:

1. Give each child a whole food. For example, a cucumber, corn in the husk, or an apple.
2. Discuss the different textures of the outside of the food—soft or hard/smooth or rough.
3. Cut open the food. Investigate the seeds. Count the seeds.
4. Pass the different foods around so each child or family member may experience the new food.
5. Use some of the seeds to plant in soil and grow in a small cup.

## Stage Three: Smell

After successfully completing the developmental stage of touching new foods, the resistant eater is now ready to smell foods and slowly bring those foods closer to the mouth. It is important to respect the child's willingness to bring a food closer to the mouth. This stage should only be implemented after the child has demonstrated mastery of touching new foods without fear or anxiety. Our sense of smell is closely linked to successful eating. Smell is an essential component of eating and can bring strong reactions. Therefore, the resistant eater may have more anxiety at this stage when bringing foods close to the mouth.

**Goals for Smelling**

- To experience a variety of smells of new foods
- To identify foods by smell from different food groups
- To produce a calming effect for the resistant eater
- To positively link smell with eating new foods

As you prepare for this stage, consider all the smells in the environment. For example, perfumes, candles and air fresheners can greatly impair a child's willingness to smell a new food item if the child is hypersensitive to strong odors. Be sure to create an environment free of extraneous smells.

**Guidelines for Implementing Stage Three-Smell**

1. **Select food items that have a calming effect on the resistant eater.** Scents such as apple, cinnamon and vanilla are much more calming than strong odors such as garlic, onion and vinegar. Start with calming and relaxing scents.

2. **Do not insist the child place a food item directly under the nose.** The olfactory system can be very sensitive and does not require direct contact with a new food. It may be more appropriate for an adult to gently wave the item in front of the child in order for her to experience the scent.

3. **Only introduce 1-3 new scents at each session.** Overloading the olfactory system can create nausea and headaches, which will have a negative effect on the child. It is better to use fewer items when implementing this stage.

### Stage Three-Smell

### Lesson 1: Food Jewelry

Materials:

- Fruits, vegetables, and other small food items
- Yarn

Procedures:

1. Cut the food items into small pieces. Using a small knife or scissors, with adult assistance, place a small hole in the food item.
2. String the food items onto the yarn.
3. Place the food necklace around the child's neck.
4. Have the child smell the food items and identify the different smells of each food.

### Lesson 2: Smelly Art

Materials:

- Scented markers, scented glue, and scented stickers
- Construction paper
- Laminating paper and laminating machine

Procedures:

1. Provide the group with a variety of art supplies that are scented. Scented markers and scented stickers are commonly available.
2. Have each member of the group make a placemat out of construction paper for the table. The placement might include pictures of favorite foods, the food pyramid, or reminders for how to create appropriate mealtime environments.
3. Discuss the scented art supplies and associate the scents with common food items.
4. Laminate the placemats for use during mealtimes.

**Lesson 3: Guess the Smell**

Materials:

- Small plastic butter tubs or empty film canisters
- 3-5 new and preferred food items

Procedures:

1. Make 3-5 small holes in the top of the container.
2. Place a food item in the container.
3. Have the child guess what item is in the container by smelling through the holes.
4. Discuss the different smells associated with foods.
5. Allow the child to select the next item to place in the plastic container.
6. Repeat several times.

## Lesson 4: Food Bingo

Materials:

- Construction paper
- 6-9 pictures of food items (pictures cut from magazines or labels from cans)
- 3x5 blank cards
- Real food items to match each picture
- Small place markers (may use plastic lids or pennies)

Procedures:

1. Determine the number of squares for the food bingo cards. Bingo cards are typically sixteen squares but smaller cards may be used.
2. Glue food pictures onto cards made out of construction paper.
3. Write the name of each food item on a 3x5 card.
4. Give each member a bingo card and several markers.
5. Turn over the 3x5 cards and select the first card.
6. Have each child identify if they have the food item on their bingo card and place a marker on the card.
7. Each time the child has a chosen food item, he or she is to hold the actual food item and smell.
8. Allow each member of the group an opportunity to select the 3x5 cards.

## Lesson 5: Matching Game

Materials:

- 3-5 food items

- 3x5 blank cards

Procedures:

1. Select 3-5 food items, including some preferred food items.
2. Write a description for each food item on a separate 3x5 card, such as: sweet, sour, bitter, strong, mild, refreshing, spicy, minty.
3. Have each member of the group smell the food item and identify which description best fits the food item.
4. Allow the children to write new and creative descriptions for each item.

## Stage Four: Taste

Although each stage of sensory development is addressed separately in this chapter, it is important to remember that a resistant eater may skip around through each stage of development. Depending on the individual child's likes and dislikes, the child may be willing to taste a new food very quickly without the necessary 10-15 positive experiences at each previous level. As mentioned earlier, the child determines the pace of the program. There may be days when the resistant eater voluntarily takes a bite of a new food but on other days the same child may be unwilling to even tolerate a new food in his vicinity. These variations in eating development are typical and should be addressed as part of the treatment plan. Not all children require the same amount or intensity of treatment.

During each of the previous stages of sensory development, the child has been consistently reassured that there is no pressure to taste or eat a new food item. Finally, in Stage Four the child is required to begin to taste a new food item.

**Goals for Tasting**

- To increase awareness of the mouth and tongue
- To provide a variety of flavors: salty, sweet, sour, and bitter
- To reduce anxiety for tasting new foods
- To provide the resistant eater with an opportunity to taste a new food without having to swallow it
- To increase the variety and number of foods the resistant eater will eat

As with all the stages of sensory development, tasting new foods should be fun and implemented without coercion. If the child has shown signs of wanting to try a new food during previous stages, be sure to include that particular food during the lessons for tasting. For example, if the child has experimented with licking a banana in a previous session, it is important to select a banana for use during the tasting sessions.

**Guidelines for Implementing Stage Four-Taste**

1. **Tasting a new food item begins with licking the item, then holding a small bite on the tongue, and finally chewing a small portion.** This stage of eating development is broken down into small teachable units.

2. **What goes in may come out!** Allow the resistant eater to spit out a new food item during the beginning lessons of Stage Four. In fact, Lesson 1 is designed to create a "spit bucket" for the child to use during future tasting experiences.

3. **Combine familiar tastes with new food items.** For example, combine a favorite sauce or condiment with a new food item to help in the transition. The resistant eater will have more success when tasting a new food if it is paired with a familiar taste.

4. **Begin by selecting new foods close in flavor and texture to preferred food items.** Small changes in preferred food items will lead to success in tasting.

5. **Include several new fruits, which are naturally sweet, to the list of new food items to taste.** A small slice of peach or banana is an excellent choice for the beginner.

6. **Select foods that are child-friendly and are comfortable for the child to chew.** Consider the texture, shape, and the overall level of eating difficulty for a given child.

7. **As the child becomes more successful with tasting new foods, begin to vary the flavors and address the range of tastes.**

8. **Have ice or water on hand for the child to use between tastes of new food.** Small chips of ice will assist in awakening the mouth and cleansing the tongue after a tasting session.

## Stage Four-Taste

### Lesson 1: Designing a Spit Bucket

Materials:

- Small plastic bucket (small paint buckets can be purchased at your local hardware store)
- Permanent markers

Procedures:

1. Provide each child with a small plastic bucket.
2. Assist the child in decorating the bucket by drawing favorite pictures. Write the child's name on the bucket.
3. On a separate piece of paper, work with the child in writing the specific rules for tasting and spitting out new foods. The child must have a clear understanding of when and where it is appropriate to spit out new foods. If the child is not following the rules regarding the "Spit Bucket," discontinue using it. The rules should be reviewed at each lesson and posted for the child to observe.
4. If the spit bucket is used in school, be sure to notify the parent of strategies for using a bucket at home.

### Lesson 2: Guess the Food

Materials:

- Blindfold
- 3-5 new and preferred food items
- "Spit Bucket"

Procedures:

The child may use the "Spit Bucket" at any time during this lesson.

1. Practice tasting the food items without the blindfold to decrease any anxiety the children may be feeling.
2. Have each child place the blindfold over their eyes, and take a small taste or lick the food item.
3. The child should attempt to guess the food item and describe the characteristics of the food. For example, the child may lick a spoonful of strawberry yogurt and describe the texture and sweetness of the yogurt.
4. Repeat this activity until everyone has had an opportunity to guess all food items.

**Lesson 3: Compare and Contrast**

Materials:

- 3-5 food items in various forms. For example, cooked vs. raw carrots; chicken nuggets vs. a chicken breast; or frozen strawberries vs. fresh strawberries.
- "Spit Bucket"

Procedures:

The child may use the "Spit Bucket" at any time during this lesson.

1. Lay out each of the food items.
2. Have each member of the group select two versions of the same food to compare and contrast.

3. Start by touching and smelling the item. When the child is ready, begin to taste the different food items.
4. Have each member of the group describe the different textures, tastes, and smells of each food item.
5. Repeat this activity until each member of the group has had an opportunity to attempt a new food.

**Lesson 4: Hide and Seek**

Materials:

- 3-5 new food items cut into small pieces
- "Spit Bucket"

Procedures:

The child may use the "Spit Bucket" at any time during this lesson.

1. This lesson is great for young children. Including music and a song will make this activity more playful and fun. For example the tune for the "Hokey Pokey" can be sung when hiding each food bite: "You put the pea in, you take the pea out, you put the pea in, and you shake it all about."
2. Have each child select a small sample of a new food item.
3. Tell the children to hide the food item in their mouth.
4. Model for the child how to place a food item under the tongue or between the cheek and gums to hide it.
5. Repeat this activity while singing a song.

## Lesson 5: Bite Art

Materials:

- 3-5 food items that are hard enough to bite (apples, carrots, cucumber, cheese, slice of lunch meat)
- "Spit Bucket"

Procedures:

The child may use the "Spit Bucket" at any time during this lesson.

1. Begin this lesson with an overview of getting to know your teeth. Discuss the different kinds of teeth and how we use them in chewing.
2. Have each child select a new food item.
3. Model for the children how our teeth can leave different bite marks or "Bite Art" in a food. For example, take an apple and gently bite into the skin. Show the group the "Bite Art."
4. Allow each child to create their own "Bite Art" and share with the group.

## Lesson 6: Cooking

Materials:

- Recipe and required food items
- Cooking utensils
- Cookbook
- Trip to the grocery store (optional)

Procedures:

1. Allow the child to select a recipe from a cookbook.

2. If possible, take the child to the grocery store to buy the necessary ingredients.
3. Make the recipe. Give the child as much independence as possible for completing this task.
4. Include other adults in tasting the new recipe.
5. Have a celebration! Decorate the setting and celebrate the child's success.

### Lesson 7: Bobbin' for Foods

Materials:

- 3-5 small food items
- Shallow serving dish or aluminum tray for each child
- "Spit Bucket"

Procedures:

1. This activity is modeled after the activity of "bobbin' for apples."
2. Place a small amount of water in each tray—one tray per child.
3. Have the child select a food item to be placed in the tray of water; for example, a raw carrot or a slice of cucumber.
4. Each child attempts to pick up the food item using their mouths only. The child may spit the food item into the bucket.
5. The game is repeated until each member of the group has sampled each food item.

## Stage Five: Eating New Foods

The last and final stage of sensory development for learning about new foods is eating. If the child has successfully completed each of the developmental stages, she is now ready to eat a balanced diet without anxiety or fear of new foods. This does not mean that the child will like every food. Goals for eating will vary depending on the age of the child and the nature of the eating problem.

**Goals for Eating**

- To enjoy a meal
- To eat a variety of foods in each food group
- To remain calm and stress-free when presented with new foods
- To be able to eat in a variety of settings

The final stage in learning about new foods will continue throughout the child's life. Parents and school personnel working with a resistant eater should maintain and return to the practical strategies outlined in the treatment plan as the child gets older and is exposed to new foods. A child who has experienced problems with eating in the past needs ongoing support throughout childhood and adolescence. It is important for the feeding team to watch for any signs that the child is regressing and requires further intervention.

## Conclusion

The lessons and strategies presented in this chapter for learning about new foods are not exhaustive. Parents or professionals working with a resistant eater can modify the lessons or create new ones based on age-appropriate fun and simple games. The lessons can be expanded if the child appears ready to take the next step. Or if there are still signs of anxiety, the child can repeat favorite lessons several times. The important aspect of each stage is to allow the child to naturally and calmly learn, without coercion, about new foods. These practical lessons along with the other treatment goals will enable resistant eaters to expand their diets and learn to love to eat appropriately.

# CHAPTER TEN

## A Recipe for Success

*It has been a year since the Jenson family began to implement an eating program for Daniel. During the last year both Daniel and his parents have learned many new strategies for addressing food aversions. Tonight's meal will be very different from a typical meal a year ago. The menu for the meal will consist of items agreed upon by the entire family. Daniel and Logan are now included in meal planning and preparation, and Daniel's father makes a point of being home for dinner during the week in order to provide the structure and predictability needed to help a resistant eater. Tonight, like many other nights in the past few months, Daniel follows a set routine of activities before dinner. He begins his routine by playing a game of basketball with his brother, which provides him with proprioceptive input to increase body awareness. After the basketball game, Daniel washes his face and hands with lukewarm water and a washcloth to desensitize his face. The washing activity helps him to feel calm and prepared for the mealtime experience. Although Daniel may still be considered a picky eater, he can now go to new restaurants without anxiety and stress for the family. He is also able to go to a friend's house for a meal. Daniel's father has changed his belief about forcing Daniel to eat, and the mealtime environment is now calm and relaxing for the entire family.*

The evening meal at the Jenson home has changed dramatically since we first read about Daniel in Chapter One. To help their son and ultimately the whole family, Daniel's parents were willing to make significant changes in their beliefs about mealtimes and who is responsible for eating. Daniel has been provided with a variety of activities to assist him in learning about new foods. Although he may never be considered a "good eater" by current societal standards, his quality of life has greatly improved after implementing a comprehensive treatment plan. He can now visit a friend's home for a meal and is less anxious around new foods. The outcome of Daniel's treatment has allowed the family to go out to new restaurants and to happily take Daniel on family vacations and holidays.

As with any individualized treatment plan, it is important to remember that several variables may impact the overall success of a program such as:

- The age of the child
- The cognitive level of the child
- Outside medical issues
- The amount and intensity of implementation across settings, including home, clinic, and school
- The use of a multidisciplinary team including teachers, therapists and parents
- The number of opportunities and experiences for the child to learn about new foods

Each of these factors may vary in the time required for positive outcomes. The goal for each individualized treatment plan is not the same for all resistant eaters.

According to parents of resistant eaters who have been through a comprehensive feeding program, there are several key components to keep in mind when looking at outcomes. The following are quotes and advice from parents of resistant eaters who have successfully completed an extensive feeding program.

"The environmental changes have made the biggest difference in our son's eating. Before the program, we never sat down as a family to eat dinner. Now, we eat together, even if it is just the two of us. I think my son watches us eating and that has made a difference. We now have a set eating schedule. My son will try new foods on his own. He does not always finish everything but at least he is trying new foods."

"Dinner time has gotten so much better since the feeding program. Before the program, if I asked my daughter to try a bite she would scream and yell. The level of stress at the dinner table was incredible. My husband and I were stressed because she wasn't eating and that made my daughter stressed. We only focused on what she ate. Now we have stopped forcing her to eat. We have stopped the battles. It has been hard, and sometimes I have to remind my husband not to try to coerce her into eating. Now that my daughter knows it is her decision whether she takes a bite or not, she is much more willing to try new foods. She has actually been eating spinach and steak. We are happier and she is happier."

"As my daughter started having more and more food aversions, I catered to her eating. I felt responsible for making sure she ate her dinner. I wish I hadn't accommodated her picky eating. It seemed the more I catered to her food demands, the worse it got. She would yell and scream if I tried to make her eat. I just gave up and made her what she wanted. Over the years we all began eating separate foods and the TV was always on during dinner. Since the feeding program has been implemented, things have really changed. We never have the TV on during dinner. I make one meal for everyone. If my daughter wants to eat, the decision is up to her. She has become much more independent in terms of eating and cleaning up after the meal."

Although the quotes and stories by the parents of former resistant eaters reflect an overwhelmingly positive experience with the eating program, certain problems may continue to interfere with the success of the program. The following are obstacles often cited by parents and professionals:

1. **Cultural Factors**

   It is important for teachers and therapists to consider the ethnicity of the resistant eater and his/her family. Often cultural beliefs will impact the nature of the mealtime environment, and particularly food selections. Cultures that are primarily vegetarian or if their diets consist of mainly soft textured foods may limit new foods to the child in order to maintain the cultural norms.

2. **Medical Issues**

   As mentioned previously, resistant eaters may have a variety of medical irregularities that interfere with their ability to acquire new foods. Severe and chronic medical issues must be addressed by a medical doctor with specialized training in eating disorders and/or gastroenterology. The side effects of the child's medications must also be reviewed for their effects on appetite and taste. Ongoing concerns related to oral-motor dysfunction and sensory integration dysfunction may require a referral to an occupational therapist for a complete assessment. For further treatment in this area, it is important to obtain a recommendation from a pediatrician or other parents who have a child with similar problems.

3. **Older Children**

The eating patterns of older children and adults with limited diets can be especially challenging as the length of time an eating problem has persisted without treatment can affect the outcomes of an otherwise effective program. For these individuals, the feeding team, including the parents, may choose to reduce the demands for eating a variety of foods and focus on other ways to maintain a healthy and nutritional diet. For example, it may be necessary to utilize supplements and vitamins to achieve maximum nutritional balance. While the overall outcomes for older children and adults may be quite different from those of younger children, a comprehensive program should be attempted as tastes will change as the child matures.

4. **Gluten, Casein, and Other Allergy-related Diets**

The lessons and strategies presented in this book can be modified to meet the needs of a child on any special diet. If the family is following a restricted diet, food selections must be in keeping with the diet. The lessons and strategies suggested in this book may be implemented according to the diet.

# Conclusion

As we near the end of our journey into the territory of new foods, we would like to leave you with some ideas for promoting a positive eating relationship. First, it is essential for those working with resistant eaters to have adequate knowledge and skills for addressing eating issues. Parents and professionals must seek out support and training in their community and strive for excellence and consistency when working with this special population. A collaborative approach within a multidisciplinary team will ensure the long-term success of the program.

Lastly, we cannot emphasize enough the importance of maintaining a well-balanced perspective when managing problems with eating. Although extremely difficult at times, parents must bear in mind the long-term goals for the child and family while minimizing the focus on day-to-day struggles that each mealtime may bring. Mistakes may have been made in the past but children are forgiving and will begin to move forward in their learning about new foods. Children have an innate ability to learn and experience new things. As parents and professionals, we must respect their gains and celebrate their successes. Happy eating!

# APPENDIX

# FOOD Guide PYRAMID

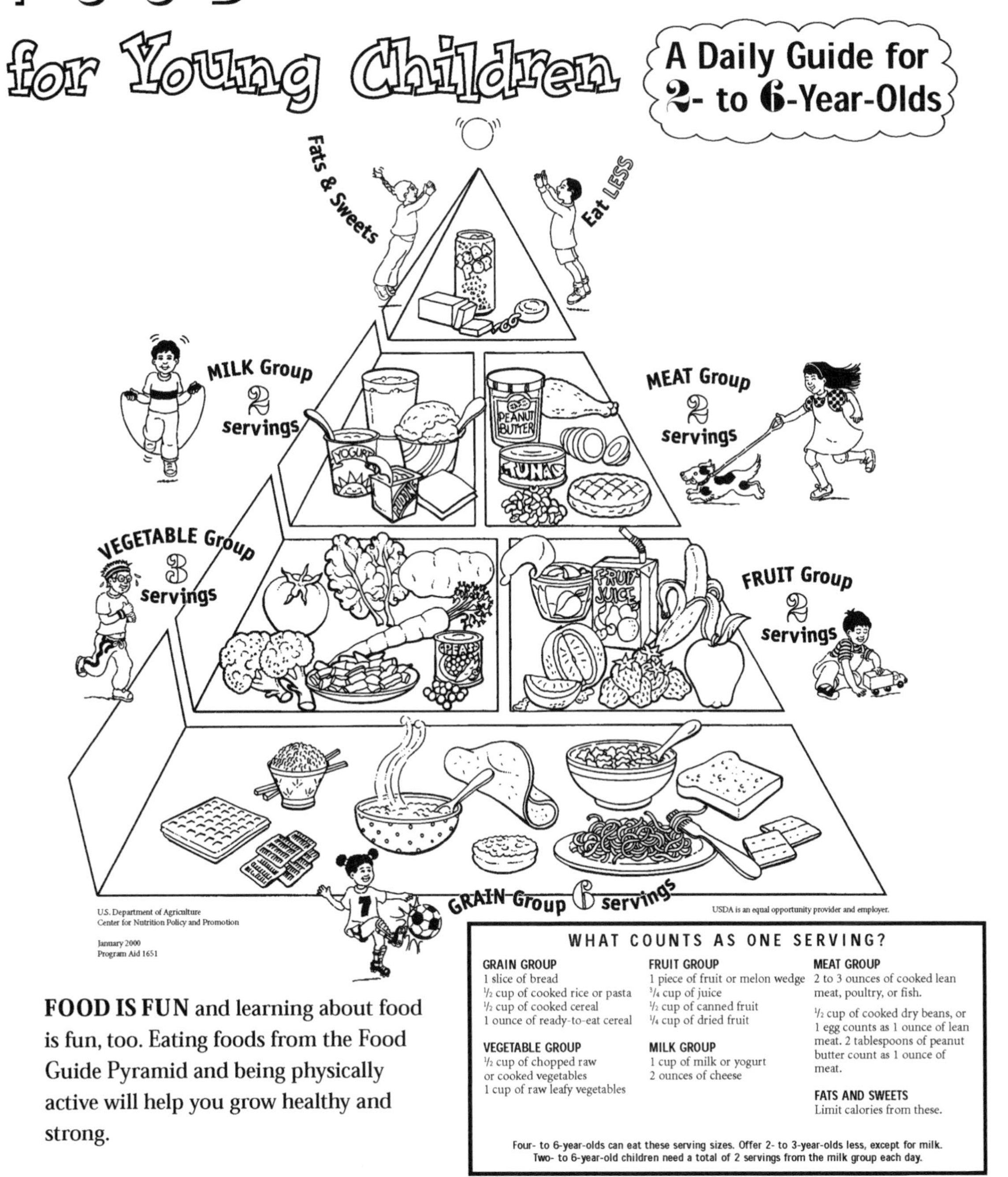


**FOOD IS FUN** and learning about food is fun, too. Eating foods from the Food Guide Pyramid and being physically active will help you grow healthy and strong.

### WHAT COUNTS AS ONE SERVING?

**GRAIN GROUP**
1 slice of bread
½ cup of cooked rice or pasta
½ cup of cooked cereal
1 ounce of ready-to-eat cereal

**VEGETABLE GROUP**
½ cup of chopped raw
or cooked vegetables
1 cup of raw leafy vegetables

**FRUIT GROUP**
1 piece of fruit or melon wedge
¾ cup of juice
½ cup of canned fruit
¼ cup of dried fruit

**MILK GROUP**
1 cup of milk or yogurt
2 ounces of cheese

**MEAT GROUP**
2 to 3 ounces of cooked lean meat, poultry, or fish.

½ cup of cooked dry beans, or 1 egg counts as 1 ounce of lean meat. 2 tablespoons of peanut butter count as 1 ounce of meat.

**FATS AND SWEETS**
Limit calories from these.

Four- to 6-year-olds can eat these serving sizes. Offer 2- to 3-year-olds less, except for milk. Two- to 6-year-old children need a total of 2 servings from the milk group each day.

## EAT a variety of FOODS AND ENJOY!

Food Pyramid: **www.usda.gov/cnpp**

## Treatment Plan

| Part 1: Environmental Controls |
|---|
| **Goal 1:** |
| Activities:<br>•<br>•<br>• |
| **Goal 2:** |
| Activities:<br>•<br>•<br>• |
| **Goal 3:** |
| Activities:<br>•<br>•<br>• |

# Treatment Plan

| Part 2: Oral-Motor/Positioning |
|---|
| **Goal 1:** |
| Activities:<br>•<br>•<br>• |
| **Goal 2:** |
| Activities:<br>•<br>•<br>• |
| **Goal 3:** |
| Activities:<br>•<br>•<br>• |

# Treatment Plan

| Part 3: Stages of Sensory Development for Eating |
|---|
| **Goal 1:** |
| Activities:<br>•<br>•<br>• |
| **Goal 2:** |
| Activities:<br>•<br>•<br>• |
| **Goal 3:** |
| Activities:<br>•<br>•<br>• |

# Cue Card Applications

*Corresponding number in Appendix:* *Page# in Text* *Page# in Appendix*

## Cue Card Applications

1.

2.

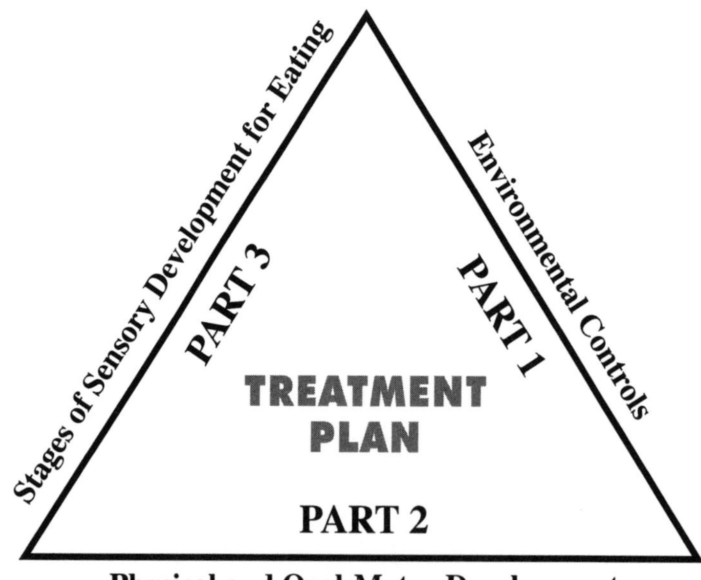

**3.**

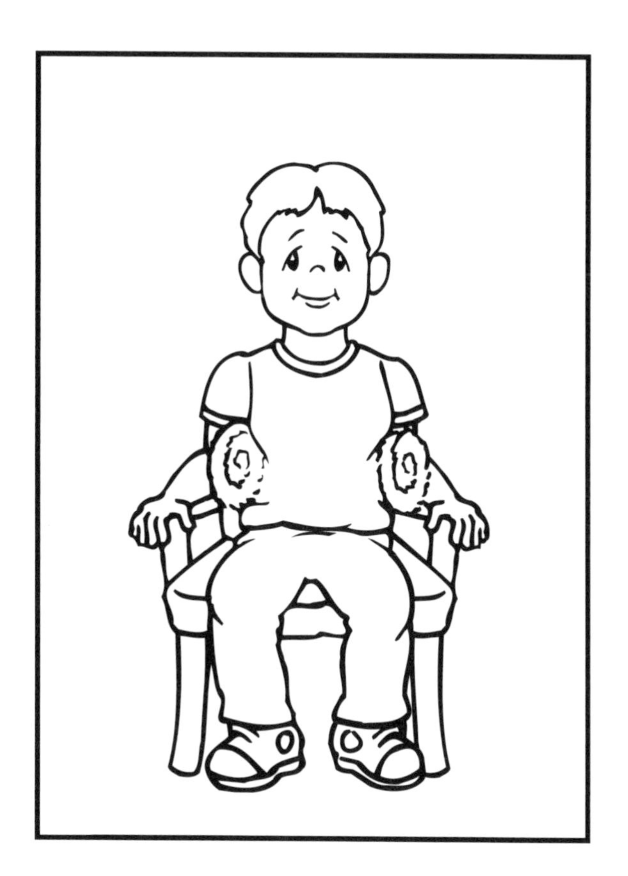

**4.**

5.

6.

7.

8.

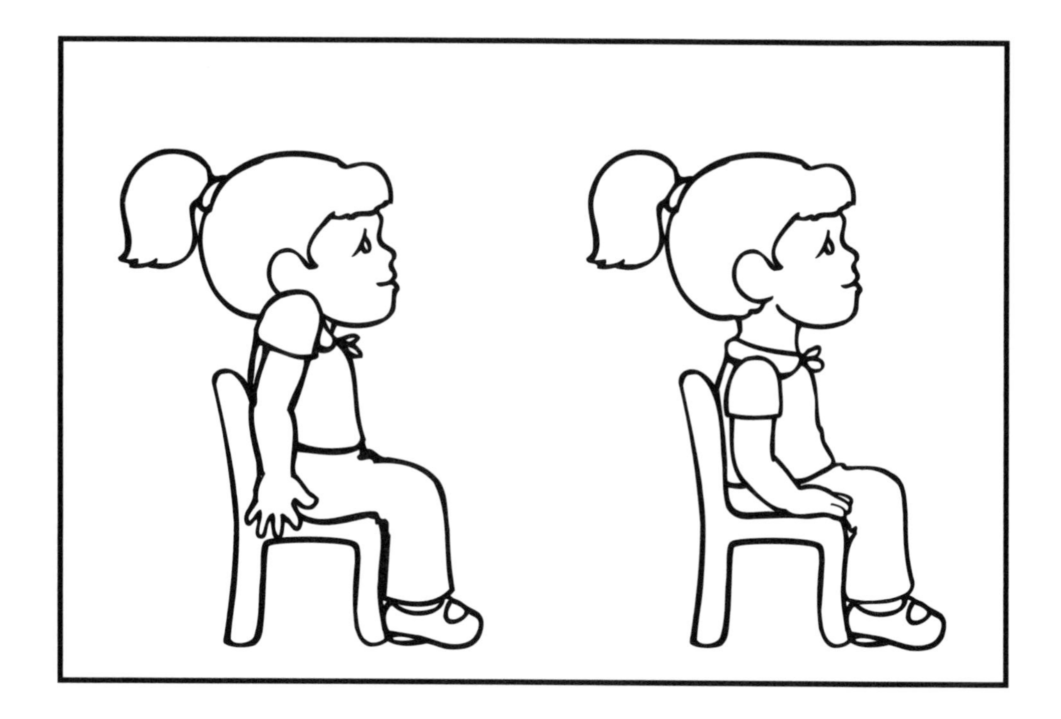

9.

10.

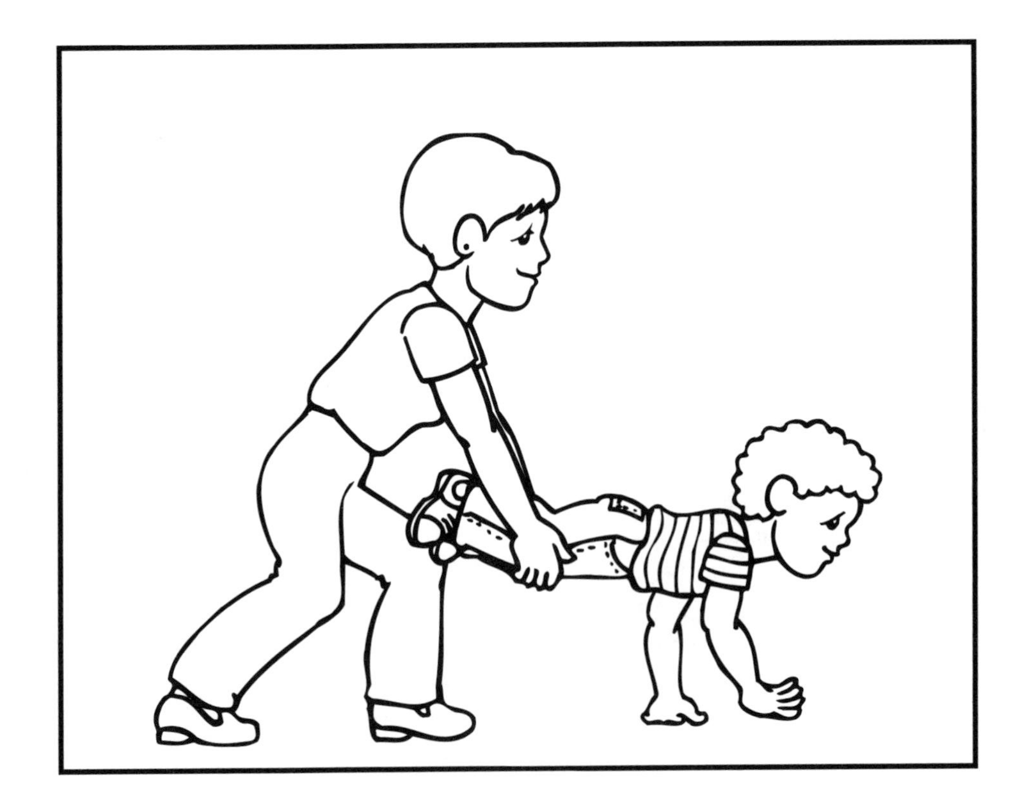

11.

12.

13.

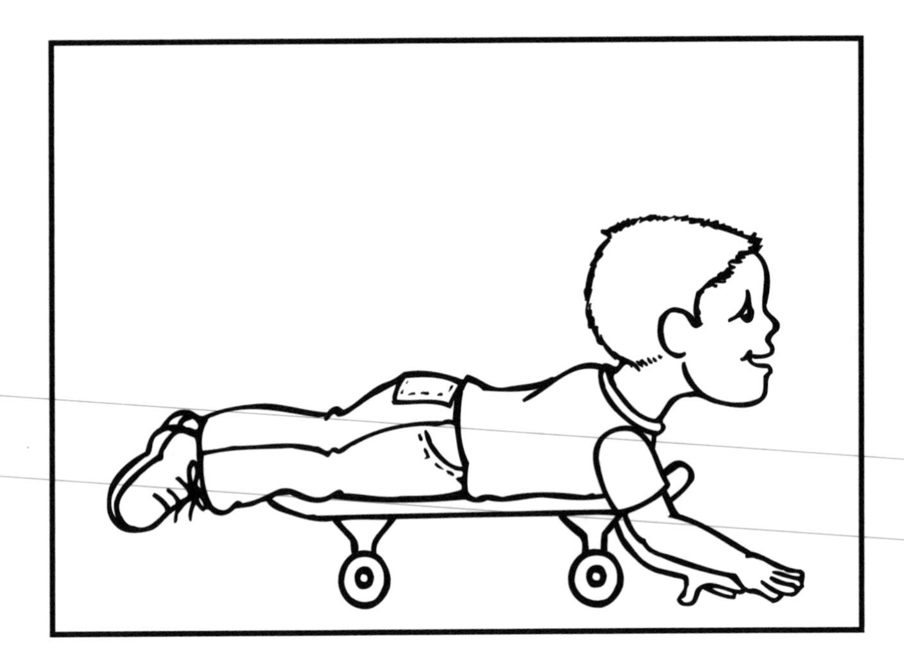

14.

**15.**

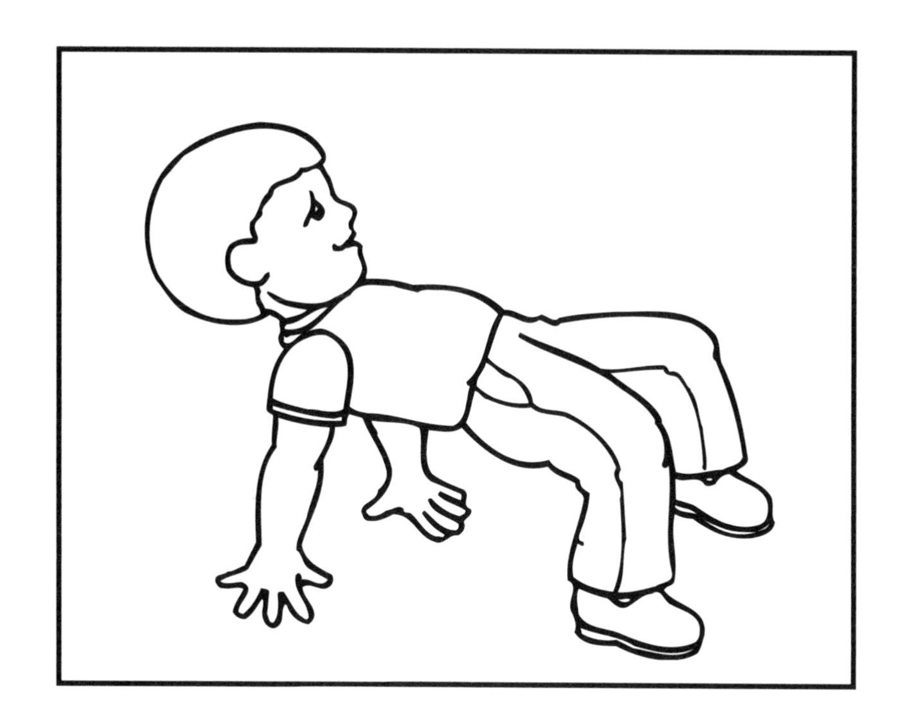

**16.**

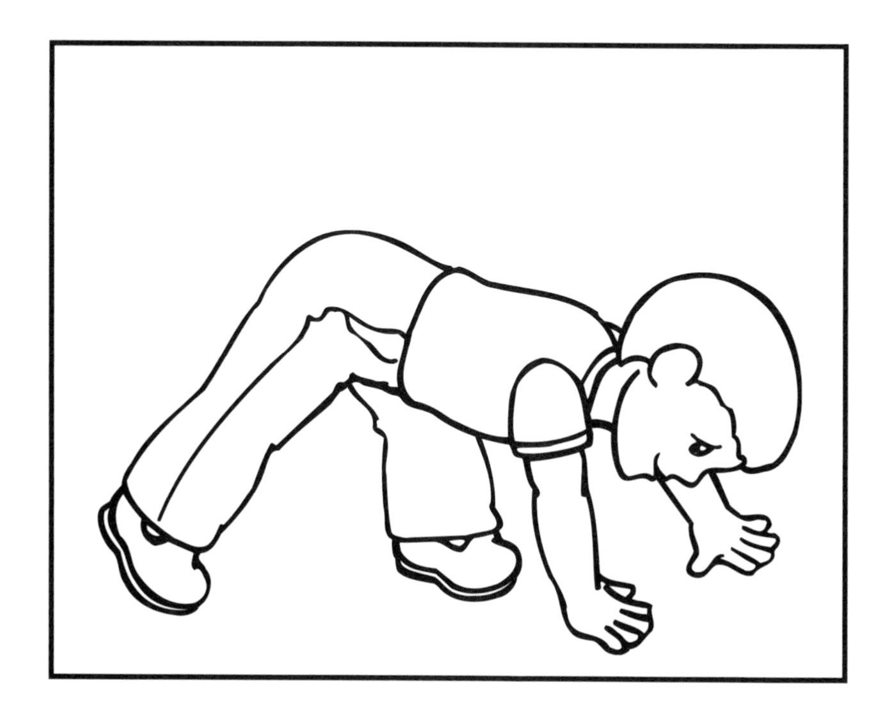

17.

18.

19.

20.

21.

22.

23.

24.

25.

26.

27.

28.

# REFERENCES

# References


Alexander, R., Boehme, R. & Cupps, B. (1993). *Normal Development of Functional Motor Skills*. The First Year of Life. Therapy Skill Builders.

Ayers, A. J. (1994). *Sensory Integration and the Child*. Western Psychological Services.

Birch, L.L. (1990). *The Control of Food Intake by Young Children: The Role of Learning in Taste, Experience, and Feeding*. Capaldi & Powley Ed. American Psychological Association.

Bly, L. (1994). *Motor Skills Acquisition in the First Year*. An Illustrated Guide to Normal Development. Therapy Skill Builders.

Cheatum, B.A. & Hammond, A.A. (2000). *Physical Activities for Improving Children's Learning and Behavior*. A Guide to Sensory Motor Development. Human Kinetics.

Hendy, H. & Raudenbush, B. (2000). *Effectiveness of Teacher Modeling to Encourage Food Acceptance in Preschool Children*. Appetite, v. 34.

Kranowitz, C.S. (1998). *The Out-Of-Sync Child*. The Berkley Publishing Group.

Kranowitz, C.S. (2003). *The Out-Of-Sync Child Has Fun*. The Berkley Publishing Group.

Kranowitz, C.S. & Szklut, S. (2001). *Answers to Questions Teachers Ask About Sensory Integration*. Sensory Resources.

Mayes & Calhoun, (1999). *Symptoms of Autism in Young Children and Correspondence with the DSM*. Infants and Young Children, v. 12.

Morris, S.E. & Klein, M.D. (2000). *Pre-Feeding Skills, A Comprehensive Resource For Mealtime Development, 2nd edition*. Therapy Skills Builders.

Money, S.S. (2002). *Where Are the Pieces?* Talk Tools.

Orr, C. (1998). *Mouth Madness*. Therapy Skills Builders.

Pliner and Hobden (1992). *Development of a Scale to Measuer the Trait of Food Neophobia in Humans*, Appetite, v.19.

Satter, E. (1987). *How to Get Your Child to Eat, But Not Too Much*. Bull Publishing.

Satter, E. (1999). *Secrets of Feeding a Healthy Family*. Kelcy Press.

Toomey, K. (2002). *When Children Won't Eat: Understanding and Preventing Feeding Problems in Children with ASD*. Presented at the Young Child with Special Needs Conference, Washington D.C.

Williams, K., Coe, D., & Snyder, A. (1998). *Use of Texture Fading in the Treatment of Food Selectivity*. Journal of Applied Behavior Analysis, v. 31.

Wing, L. (2001). *The Autistic Spectrum: A Parent's Guide to Understanding and Helping Your Child*. Ulysses Press.

Yack, E., Sutton, S. & Aquilla, P. (1998). *Building Bridges Through Sensory Integretion*. Syd and Ellen Lerer.

## Additional Resources Available from Dr. Lori Ernsperger

***Keys to Success for Teaching Students with Autism*** (Future Horizons, Inc. 2003)

This book offers school personnel a practical guide for educating students with autism. This resource unlocks the secrets of six critical teaching elements: effective classroom environments, curriculum development, instructional strategies, managing problem behaviors, data collection, and building collaborative teams. Regardless of their level of experience, teachers now have a book which allows them to create and implement effective educational programs.

## Staff Development and Parent Training

Dr. Ernsperger provides intensive training to small and large groups utilizing a variety of formats. Workshop and conference topics include:

- Identifying an Appropriate Curriculum for Students with Autism Spectrum Disorders
- Implementing Effective Instructional Strategies including Applied Behavior Analysis and Discrete Trial Instruction
- Proactive Strategies for Managing Problem Behaviors and Developing Reinforcement Strategies
- Practical Strategies for Including Students with Asperger's Syndrome
- How to Get Your Child to Eat a Balanced Diet and Taming Mealtime Battles

For additional information, call Dr. Ernsperger (702) 616-8717 or e-mail: drlori@cox.net.

## Websites

U.S. Department of Agriculture: **www.usda.gov.** Includes free posters and food pyramid workbooks.

Dole Food Company: **www.5aday.com.** Provides a catalogue of activities and posters on healthy eating topics.

North American Society for Pediatric Gastoenterology, Hepatology and Nutrition: **www.naspgn.org.**

Pediatric/Adolescent Gastroesophageal Reflux Association: **www.reflux.org**

Sensory Integration: **www.sinetwork.org**

Out-Of-Sync Child: **www.out-of-sync-child.com**

Food Pyramid: **www.usda.gov/cnpp**